JOHN PAUL II

JOHN PAUL II

✝

A Personal Portrait
of the Pope and the Man

RAY FLYNN

WITH

ROBIN MOORE & JIM VRABEL

St. Martin's Press ❧ New York

www.stmartins.com

ISBN 0-312-26681-2

First Edition: April 2001

10 9 8 7 6 5 4 3 2 1

*This book is dedicated to all those
who suffer from depression and mental illness,*

*but because of their faith in God,
have found peace and hope.*

CONTENTS

ACKNOWLEDGMENTS

This book is the result of years of observation, study, and a personal friendship with Pope John Paul II. At the outset, I would like to offer my thanks, deepest admiration, and respect to two very talented and thoughtful men—noted best-selling author Robin Moore and soon-to-be-recognized writer Jim Vrabel.

I also want to thank my wife, Kathy; our children, Ray Jr., Eddie, Julie, Nancy, Katie, and Maureen; our grandchild, James; sons-in-law, Mike Degulis and Jamie Long; and soon-to-be son-in-law, Mike Foley; and their wonderful families. Thanks to Robin Moore's wife, Mary Olga; and Jim Vrabel's wife, Eiric, and his daughter, Zoe, for letting them put in so much time on this project. Special thanks to Kristen Hansen for her professional assistance.

My thanks go also to the many Vatican and U.S. church officials for the insights and friendship they shared with me over the years, especially the late John Cardinal O'Connor and Giuseppe Cardinal Caprio. My admiration to Cardinal Secretary of State Angelo Sodano, Secretary for Relations with States Archbishop Jean-Louis Tauran, and Prefect for Social Communication Archbishop John Foley; Bernard Cardinal Law, Francis Cardinal George, and William Cardinal Baum; Bishops Stanislaw Dziwisz, James Harvey, Dino Monduzzi; Monsignor Stanislaw Sypeck; and Revs. Robert Graham, S.J., John Farren, O.P., and James Quigley, O.P. Also, appreciation to Monsignor Robert J. Dempsey, who heads up the English edition of *L'Osservatore Romano*.

I want to express special thanks to the Monsignor Tim Dolan, and to all the staff and students at the North American College in Rome for the friendship, instruction, conversation, and the good meals I enjoyed with them at the campus on the Gianicolo Hill. I also want to thank Monsignor George Higgins of Catholic University, whose commitment to social and economic justice is a source of enormous inspiration, and the Rev. Richard Shmaruk for his careful reading of this manuscript and thoughtful advice. Thanks to labor leader Ken Lyons of N.A.G.E. (National Association of Government Employees) for his friendship, American Catholic Television, Dr. Alfred Arcidi, and the good people of Boston who have always been there for me these many years.

My thanks to the Mel and Charlene Graham family for sharing their son, Marty, with all of us, and to Charlene Bizokas for allowing me to tell her story. I want to express my thanks to Hall of Fame shortstop Phil Rizzuto—a big fan of John Paul II—and to Gilbert Levine, Joan Lewis of Vatican Information Service, Cindy Wooden of Catholic News Service, Tad Szulc, Ambassador Steve Falaz, Ted Buzcko, Catholic Alliance attorneys Dennis Lynch and Phil Moran, Doc Tynan, Evelyn Rolak, John W. McCormack, Mike Sheehan, John Alberts, John Stinson, and my family in Cork, Galway, and Kerry for sharing their insights with me. I also want to thank my staff at the U.S. Vatican Embassy in Rome, especially Mirella Giacolone and Claudio Manno for their support during my tenure as U.S. Ambassador, and to thank all of the many friends we made in Rome, especially the dedicated nuns and priests we got to know so well. My family's naturally friendly demeanor gave me the opportunity to meet so many wonderful new families while living in Italy—an experience we'll forever value.

At St. Martin's Press, I want to thank senior editor Diane Higgins for her faith in this project, and her assistants, Patty Fernandez, Nichole Argyres, and Joan Higgins, for all their help. Our thanks also go to Mel Berger of the William Morris Agency, and to attorneys John Moore and Harry Grill.

Finally, I want to thank Karol Wojtyla, John Paul II, a courageous leader for not only inspiring me and lifting the spirits of my family, but for inspiring and lifting the spirits of so many people all around the world.

*A personal description of the pope—from someone
who had a front-row seat*

I want to start by taking the unusual step of describing what this book *isn't*. This book *isn't* a biography of John Paul II, one that takes you from his boyhood in the small Polish town of Wadowice, through his college days under the Nazis and his years as a priest under the Communists, and on to his papacy. Even if he'd never become pope, Karol Wojtyla's life story would make a great book and an even better movie, but I'll leave that for others to try and capture.

This book *isn't* an analysis of John Paul II's papacy, either, nor is it an assessment of whether his tenure as pope strengthened the Catholic Church or made it more rigid, whether he has attracted people or turned them away. That's for theologians and Church historians to decide. This *isn't* a book that seeks to describe the political role John Paul II has played in the twentieth century or an attempt to define him as a "conservative" or a "liberal," oversimplified American political terms that just don't work when trying to describe this pope. This book doesn't seek to fix John Paul II's place in history, either, although his role in helping to force the fall of communism certainly places him at the top of twentieth-century world leaders.

This book *isn't* any of those things. Instead, it *is* a profile of John Paul II as a pope, a priest, and a man based on close observation and the moments I spent in his presence over the last thirty years, from the time I first met a relatively obscure Polish cardinal in a church hall in

Boston until my most recent encounter with "John Paul the Great" on the steps of St. Peter's Basilica in Rome.

I've had the opportunity to observe him and talk with him many times. I've seen him kiss babies and listen patiently to elderly people with long stories to tell him. I've seen him with the homeless and with Gypsy families, with princes and kings. I've seen him stare down politicians and tell crowds of thousands of people things they didn't particularly want to hear. I've watched him exchange high fives with young people and quietly minister to parents in pain. I've heard him make jokes and watched him deeply in prayer. And I came to admire him for all his qualities—his wide and deep intelligence, his comic timing and dramatic flair, his understanding of political realities, and his refusal to compromise morality. At a time when we in the United States have had such a difficult time in choosing a leader, it is clearer than ever to me how blessed we all have been in the leadership provided by John Paul II to the Catholic Church and the world for more than twenty-two years.

I'm not a biographer, a theologian, or a historian. But just as Tad Szulc, one of John Paul's many biographers, says that you have to be Polish to understand the Polish-ness of this pope, I think my background and experience give me a unique perspective from which to paint this portrait of John Paul II as both a public figure and a man of God. I'm a working-class, Catholic politician—and because of that I think I understand certain things about Karol Wojtyla, and the life he has led and the role he has played on the world stage.

"Do not be afraid," he has said over and over again—from the time he was chosen pope and went before a crowd of Romans in St. Peter's Square as the first Polish pope; to the historic return to his homeland, still under Communist rule; to his missions to the United States, where he reminded us that with freedom and wealth come responsibility; to his many trips around the world preaching the need for truth and for respecting the dignity of the human person. It is because he has not been afraid to speak the truth that I have come to admire and respect him so much as a pope. It is because he has been so kind to me, to my family, and to ordinary people that I have come to be so grateful to him as a priest and a man.

No single book can capture so vast a personality and complex a character as that of John Paul II. This book is not an attempt to define John Paul II so much as it is an effort to describe the man I came to not only admire and respect, but also to love.

John Paul II

FIRST IMPRESSIONS

A Polish cardinal talks about dockworkers in a church in Boston

The first time I met Karol Wojtyla was in September 1969. I was running for public office—state representative from South Boston, Massachusetts—for the first time, and I got a call from a friend of mine, Joe Aleks, who was very active in Boston's Polish American community.

"Ray," he said, "they're having a time down at St. Adalbert's in Hyde Park on Sunday. If you want to get the Polish vote, you oughta be there." Before I had a chance to ask any questions, Joe hung up. But I had enough confidence in his political instincts that when Sunday came around I headed out to St. Adalbert's.

A "time" in Boston political, social, and religious circles is any event or reception that is held to honor someone—living or dead. People are judged by whose "times" they attend, just as the person being honored is judged by the attendance at their "time." It was only when I got to St. Adalbert's that evening that I found out that this "time" was being held for the Archbishop of Kraków, the first Polish cardinal ever to visit the United States.

I have to admit, I didn't know anything about the guest of honor. But I did know the person hosting the event, Richard Cardinal Cushing of Boston. Like me, Cushing had been born and raised in "Southie" (South Boston). When I was a kid, I sold him his newspaper from my spot at the corner of Broadway and Dorchester Street in Andrew Square and I remembered that when Archbishop Cushing was made cardinal, everybody in the neighborhood was so proud that one of our own had become a prince of the church. As the years went by everybody in the whole city of Boston came to love the gravel-voiced, craggy-faced archbishop, famous for his wisecracks and for mixing politics and religion.

During the Mass that preceded the reception that evening, Cardinal Cushing gave the guest of honor a warm welcome. He praised Cardinal Wojtyla's strong leadership in Poland during "this difficult hour." He talked about how Wojtyla was close to the "working classes" because he had worked in a chemical factory as a young man. He told those attending the Mass about the cardinal's standing up to the Communist government and getting the first church in the new "worker's city" of Nowa Huta. Turning to look at his Polish colleague, he also described how students and intellectuals flocked to him by the thousands.

I was impressed by Cardinal Cushing's introduction of this Polish cardinal. I was even more impressed by what I heard afterward, at the reception, while I was waiting on the line to meet him. "He's quite a guy," one of the priests from Our Lady of Czestochowa parish in South Boston told me. "They say he was in the Polish underground during the war. Afterward, he was a theology and philosophy teacher before he became a bishop."

I began to pay more attention to this special visitor. He was a handsome, solidly built man with a wide, open face and clear eyes. There was a kind of glow, a shining look that emanated from his face. He seemed comfortable "working the room," as we call it in politics. He stood at the end of the receiving line in the parish hall after some priests, monsignors and bishops and next to Cushing. As people came up, he'd speak to them, sometimes in Polish, sometimes in English.

"How are you? Good to meet you. Good to see you," I heard him say to people ahead of me as I waited to be introduced to him. Some people—politicians, priests, celebrities—aren't really all that comfortable with the "pressing the flesh" side of the business, but this guy seemed to like it.

When it came my turn to meet this Cardinal Wojtyla, Cardinal

Cushing introduced me by saying, "Your Eminence, this is one of my neighbors from South Boston, Ray Flynn. Ray was a good athlete in school, a basketball player." The cardinal from Poland nodded his head to show he understood. "An athlete?" he said. "I was a soccer player myself."

Then Cushing, as if thinking of something less trivial and more appropriate to say, added, "Ray's father is a dockworker. He helps us run the Communion breakfasts. Sometimes we get a thousand people at them." The Boston cardinal was referring to the annual Communion breakfast at St. Vincent de Paul Church. Back then, before containerization and automation, thousands of men made their living on the docks of the port of Boston, and many priests worked closely with them, not just in religious issues but on issues of employment, working conditions, and wages. It was very much like the world captured in the movie *On the Waterfront,* where Karl Malden portrays a priest who tries to help keep the dockworkers' union from being taken over by gangsters.

Cardinal Wojtyla was shaking my hand when Cardinal Cushing made the comment about my father, and the Polish cardinal wouldn't let go. He squeezed it as if he recognized a connection, as if we had something in common. "Dockworkers," he said, in his halting English. "Much work . . . very difficult . . . not safety on the ships."

I was startled by his words. I knew all about the "not safety," the dangerous conditions. My father had gone to our parish priest for help when he and his fellow workers suffered bites from the spiders and other insects that attached themselves to the animal hides they unloaded from South America. My wife's father, who was also a dockworker, had been injured when a roll of sheet steel had fallen on his leg. After that, he was never able to work again. I had worked on the docks myself, alongside my father—until he convinced me to go to college and find a different line of work. I was surprised that this Polish cardinal would comment on the dockworker's life, but I shouldn't have been. Years later, I would discover that Father Wojtyla's first published article, in the Polish Catholic weekly *Tygodnik Powszechny* in 1949, concerned the worker-priest movement on the docks of Marseilles in France.

I would have liked to talk more with the guest of honor. But it was time for me to move on. There was a long line behind me. As I left him, I heard one of the priests introduce the next person in line, an older woman from the parish. ". . . and this is Mrs. . . . , Your Eminence. She made the dumplings." As he said this, the priest pointed to the table on the other side of the room overflowing with various dishes of Polish food. The smell of it all—the *kielbasa, kapusta,* and *golumbki*—brought back memories of growing up in the Polish section of South Boston around Andrew Square before my family moved to an area called City Point. It obviously brought back memories for our special guest, too.

"The Polish in America have not forgotten how to cook," Cardinal Wojtyla said. "It is all good. Too good!" he said, patting his stomach. "My clothes won't fit me when I get back to Kraków." Everyone laughed at the cardinal's joke, including the cardinal himself. Once again I was surprised. Most of the Polish priests I knew from Our Lady of Czestochowa and other parishes were more reserved and much less outgoing. This guy was more like an Irish priest in the way he interacted with people and joked around, even with people he had never met.

Somebody brought a baby to be blessed, and the cardinal took it willingly and confidently, not like a lot of priests I'd seen, who were nervous when handling babies. Cardinal Wojtyla held up the baby and made faces at it and got the child to laugh. The cardinal didn't seem self-conscious, didn't seem to take himself too seriously. Cardinal Cushing looked on, approvingly, since Cushing himself loved to clown around and wear funny hats. This Polish cardinal seemed to have that same confidence and sense of humor. He also appeared to have a kind of inner peace about him, a serenity. He wasn't rushing anybody. He talked to people as long as they had something to say. He didn't just nod to them while looking beyond them to the next person in line. And when he was done with one person, he accorded the next person the same special treatment, as if he or she were the only one in the room. The cardinal didn't appear to be in a hurry. He seemed glad to be there, in that room, in that part of the world. He seemed comfortable, as though he were part of the family. As a would-be politician who was still not all that comfortable in these kinds of settings, I realized I could learn something from this guy.

"Yes, and where are you from? Where is your family from?" Cardinal Wojtyla asked person after person in the line. "When did they come? Do you write to them? Have you ever been back?" When someone said they were from Kraków, I saw the cardinal's eyes light up. "What's the name again?" He would ask, and "where does your family live?" He didn't just ask one question, he posed follow-up queries. He seemed like an uncle from Poland who hadn't seen the rest of his family, those who had come to America, in many years.

"How old?" he asked someone who brought children up to meet him. Then, bending down to the kids: "Do you like school? Do you study hard?" Then, standing up and talking to the parents again, he said, "Do you teach them Polish? It is good for children to know their language. And to know God loves them."

In South Boston, we frequently had visitors, including priests and bishops, from Ireland. Many people in the neighborhood still had family in the *Auld Sod* and visited back and forth all the time. I remember thinking, after I had already gone through the receiving line and was standing off to the side, how different it must be for Polish Americans. They couldn't go back and forth that easily. I didn't know what the rules were about writing letters or sending money. Many Polish Americans were founding prosperous, middle-class families in this generation. I didn't know if they could share their prosperity with their families back in Communist Eastern Europe. I made a mental note to find out more about what they were going through.

The reception continued. It was very informal, very lighthearted, as if everyone was taking a cue from the guest of honor. A band began to play polka music. People were laughing. Children were running around underfoot. It was more like a wedding reception than a party for a visiting church dignitary. I took advantage of the opportunity to talk with all my old neighbors and remind them I was running for state representative. But I keep looking over my shoulder at this visiting cardinal. I remember wondering how America must seem to him. When this was all over we'd get in our cars and drive back home, get up tomorrow morning, and go to work in a free country—and take it all for granted. Life must have been so different for him, growing up under the Nazis and then becoming a priest under a Communist regime.

I remember wishing I had more time to talk to this Cardinal Wojtyla, to ask him more questions. I was intrigued by him. There was something special about him. I didn't know he would go on to become pope, of course, but, even so, I wished I could get to know him better. Little did I know I would have the chance.

2

A POLISH POPE IN ROME

And a celebration in South Boston

Almost ten years went by. I heard Cardinal Wojtyla's name mentioned once in a while in Boston's Polish community, and saw his picture occasionally in some of the Polish newspapers, but I don't think I ever noticed a mention of him in the "mainstream" press. That is, until October 16, 1978, when the whole world heard his name and he became John Paul II, the first Polish pope.

I heard the news on my car radio as I was driving home from a meeting at City Hall and knew enough to head directly for the Polish area of South Boston. As a state legislator, I had represented the area, but my ties went much farther back than that. I had been born in the neighborhood, on Boston Street, right around corner from our Lady of Czestochowa church and right next to the Polish American Citizens Club. In fact, my christening had been held at the P.A.C. We lived so close to it that my mother handed me through the window of our house to my aunt who had already gone next door to the party.

Upon entering politics, I kept up my connection there. On Saturdays, I'd hold "office hours" at the P.A.C., setting up a table right next to one used by people collecting donations for the Polish relief society. I would also attend the annual installation of the officers of the P.A.C. and the Kosciusko American Legion Post, and the wreath-laying ceremony in front of the statue of General Thaddeus Kosciusko—Polish patriot and hero of the American Revolution—that stands in the Boston Public Garden.

On this particular day, as I drove into the Polish neighborhood, I saw that people already had heard the news. They were pouring out of their houses, wanting to share their joy, wanting to be together, wanting to celebrate. With no public square in which to congregate as they might have done back in Poland, they streamed from all directions toward the church of Our Lady of Czestochowa on Dorchester Avenue. At the statue of Our Lady in front of the church, they placed piles of red and white flowers, the colors of Poland. They also piled flowers in front of the portrait of the Black Madonna inside.

I entered the church, which was rapidly filling up. People knelt in prayer. Old women, kerchiefs on their heads, said the rosary as tears of joy lined their faces. There were plenty of men in the church, too. Unlike some other groups, the Polish men didn't leave God for the women only. Looking around the church, I recognized a number of other local politicians, many who I'd never seen in this part of town before. Today, though, everybody wanted to be Polish.

The priests of the parish quickly organized and celebrated a Mass of Thanksgiving. In his homily, the pastor reminded us of the new pope's visit to Boston when he was a cardinal. I thought back to the brief time I'd spent with him, and the deep impression he'd made on me. Evidently, I realized, I wasn't the only one he impressed. The pastor also talked about the history of Poland, and how, like that of the Catholic Church, it was rooted in suffering and pain. Sometimes, though, he said, there were events like today when God gives us a cause for extraordinary joy and hope. When it came time to sing, people joined in with so much gusto that they almost took the roof off the church.

After Mass, people poured outside and stood milling around on the sidewalk. It seemed as if no one wanted to go home, no one wanted the evening to end. To accommodate the people's need to celebrate together, the priests opened up a function room in St. Mary's School, right around the corner on Boston Street. Coffee and cookies were brought in and the celebration continued.

Today, my daughter Maureen teaches at St. Mary's, and she says some of the nuns and people who work at the school still talk about that day, the way Red Sox fans talk about the team winning the 1967 pennant. In both cases, it was the fulfillment of what seemed like an impossible dream.

Paul Wolon, a Boston police officer, and his wife Magdalene, lived in the first floor of a three-decker right across the street from the church, and they invited a bunch of us back to their place for an impromptu house party. Magdalene opened up a big Krakus Polish ham, and started making sandwiches for everyone. Paul brought out the Polish beer. I remember that Paul's mother, who lived there too, had the biggest collection of porcelain figures—Hummels, I think they're called—that I ever saw. That night, sitting in the living room, surrounded by her Hummels, and by a bunch of her women friends who, like her, were immigrants to this country, she prayed the rosary while Polish music played on the record player.

Just when it seemed that the house party was winding down, Joe Szep, president of the Polish American Citizens Club, called to say that the band had just started playing and that everyone was invited to come over to the P.A.C. We all took him up on his offer, including Mrs. Wolon and her cronies, and beer flowed and polka music played long into the night.

Years later, I had the opportunity to tell John Paul II about the celebration that took place in South Boston when he was named pope. A playful smile crossed his face, and the Holy Father said to me: "You told me what time the party started—but not when it came to an end."

3

FIRST PAPAL VISIT TO THE UNITED STATES

Returning to Boston, "John Paul Superstar" takes the city by storm

Our second meeting took place ten years later, in October 1979. By then Cardinal Wojtyla had become Pope John Paul II, and he'd taken the world by storm with his outgoing personality, outspoken nature, and willingness to reach out to Catholics and non-Catholics in his travels all over the world.

The still-new pope had already made his triumphant visit to Poland, where the Communist regime had to sit back and watch as millions of Polish people turned out to welcome their favorite son home. Now he was coming to America directly from Ireland, where he had become the first pope to visit the Emerald Isle. *Time* magazine was calling him "John Paul Superstar," and Boston was the first stop on his American "tour" that would draw huge crowds wherever he went.

I managed to meet the pope twice on his one-day visit, the first time as a politician, the second as a parishioner. Since our last meeting, I had won my first campaign for public office and five more since. Now I was a Boston City Councillor, and so part of the welcoming delegation of political, religious, and civic leaders who met the pope's Aer Lingus plane, the *St. Patrick,* at Logan International Airport. When John Paul II appeared in the doorway of the plane, I recognized the square, solid features of the Polish cardinal I'd met ten years earlier in the parish hall of a Boston church. I had noticed something special about him then. Now there was an additional aura about him, that of someone who knew he was being watched by everyone and had to perform the role expected of him. I watched him solemnly descend the steps of the plane, ceremoniously kneel down to kiss the ground of the runway, then rise and graciously accept the greetings of the welcoming delegation, beginning with First Lady Rosalynn Carter and Humberto Cardinal Medeiros, who had succeeded the late Cardinal Cushing as Archbishop of Boston.

When it came my turn to shake hands with the pope and kiss his ring, I saw that even though he had assumed the trappings and demands of his new office, he hadn't changed that much in ten years. He still had the same wide, open face, the same engaging smile. He looked a little tired, probably from the three days he'd spent touring Ireland and the six-hour plane ride, and with all the people around him, the cameras and photographers, it was understandable that he didn't seem to have that same degree of serenity that had struck me when I met him at St. Adalbert's. I wanted to say something to him, something that might re-establish the connection that I'd felt with him back then—but there really wasn't time and it wasn't the right place.

There was a brief welcoming ceremony. Mrs. Carter praised the pope's attempt to "reach out to the world," and when it was the pope's turn to speak, he underscored that commitment, saying that he regretted that he couldn't accept all the invitations from "religious and civil officials, by individuals, families and groups"—but even though he wasn't able to meet "every man and woman, to caress every child in whose eyes is reflected the innocence of love . . . still I feel close to all of you and you are all in my prayers." And the way he said it— looking up and into the faces of people as he finished his litany—you felt he meant it.

After the ceremony, the pope got into his car and the motorcade into Boston began. I rode along behind, in a bus full of priests, monsignors, and bishops from all over New England. As we followed the pope's car through Boston's neighborhoods, we saw throngs of people who had turned out to see this dynamic young pope from Poland. They were lining the sidewalks, five or ten deep, waving, cheering, holding signs and banners, and singing songs. It was a far cry, I thought, from his visit ten years earlier when only the people of the Polish parishes turned out to welcome him.

I had to skip the next event, a prayer service at Boston's Cathedral of the Holy Cross, because I was scheduled to "work" at the stop after that. John Paul II was going to celebrate Mass at Boston Common, the oldest public park in America. A huge altar had been set up there facing Beacon Hill and the gold-domed Massachusetts State House. Here—as everywhere he visited—the pope had asked that his "special friends," those with physical or mental handicaps, be provided special access to him. My wife, Kathy, and I and other members of our parish at St. Augustine had volunteered to help Father Thomas McDonnell assist people with disabilities in getting out of their vans and buses and to their places up at the front of the stage.

When I arrived at the Common, I saw that two million people had filled it to overflowing. It was the largest crowd in Boston history, the largest crowd I had ever seen. I found Kathy and the other members of our group and got to work. Just as we got everyone settled, the pope's motorcade came into sight. People cheered from one end of the Common to another, the noise rolling like thunder under the gray, threatening skies. We watched as the pope's limousine pulled into the underground parking garage below Boston Common, where a mobile home had been brought in for the pope to use as a place to change into his vestments for the outdoor Mass.

It turned out that in addition to providing special access for the handicapped, this pope also went out of his way to thank all the volunteers who made his big, outdoor events possible. A few minutes before the Mass was to start, a group of us were called to a backstage area. After a short wait, a curtain opened and John Paul II came out from behind it. He made his way along the line of volunteers, shaking hands and blessing us. The fatigue and the tension I saw at the airport seemed to have faded now. I was struck again by how at ease he was meeting people. He tried to say something to everyone, mostly "Thank you," or "A lot of work, I know," or "I appreciate." Once again, though, he didn't seem to rush, even though two million people were waiting for him on the other side of the canvas.

When he came to my place in the line, I kissed his ring, and this time I did take the opportunity to speak to him. "It is good to see you again, Holy Father," I said.

"Again?" He looked surprised.

"I met you once before, on your first visit to Boston, in 1969."

Now, the pope smiled in recognition. "St. Adalbert's . . . Cardinal Cushing," he said.

I was impressed by his memory and his quick recall. I introduced him to Kathy and the pope blessed the two of us, and then made his way down the rest of the line, at one point glancing up at the threatening sky. When he finished, he went back behind the canvas and Kathy and I and the others rejoined the people we had helped to seat in the front section of the audience.

When the pope came out onto the stage, he was greeted by a thunderous ovation from the huge crowd. Thousands of red and white balloons were released into the dark sky, and the choir began singing. Just before he started to celebrate Mass, the pope walked down to the front of the stage and gave a special blessing to our group of handicapped people. They were all beaming, their faces turned upward, all focused on the pope's every move. Some had rosaries wrapped around their hands, some were crying. But they all seemed lost to everything except this moment, when a pope—this pope—came to them, knowing that they couldn't easily go to him.

During the Mass, I was struck by how precise and dramatic the pope's movements were as he made his way around the altar. Any regular churchgoer knows that some priests can be somewhat mechanical in officiating Mass, not because the physical acts of the service have little meaning for them but because the words mean so much more. This pope, though, seemed to combine the whole package, to convey as much with his movements as with his words. It was gripping just to watch him make his sacred rounds.

The Holy Father delivered his homily. For me, and for the group I was with, the highlight came when he said, "I greet all Americans without distinction. I want to meet you and tell you all—men and women of all creeds and ethnic origins, children and youth, fathers and mothers, the sick and the elderly—that God loves you. That he has given you a dignity as human being that is beyond compare. I want to tell everyone that the pope is your friend."

His words provoked another thunderous response from the crowd, after which many of them started chanting "Long live the pope! Long live the pope!" When the chanting stopped and the pope was able to continue, he paid tribute to the history of the United States—but also called for a "more just and humane future." When he said the words "I greet you, America the beautiful!" the crowd erupted again with applause, and again began chanting, this time in Italian, "Viva il papa! Viva il papa!"

The pope waited, then went on. He repeated his "deep regret that I am unable to accept all the invitations. I would willingly make a pastoral visit everywhere if it were possible." Then he turned his attention to young people, pleading with them to follow Christ. He ended his homily with a litany that included everyone: "Follow Christ! You who are married . . . follow Christ! You who are single . . . follow Christ! You who are young or old . . . follow Christ! You who are sick or aging, who are suffering or in pain; you who feel the need for healing, the need for love, the need for a friend . . . follow Christ! This is why I have come to America, and why I have come to Boston tonight. To call you to Christ—to call all of you and each of you to live in His love, today and forever. Amen!"

The only thing that even remotely spoiled the day occurred when the threatening skies finally opened and the rain poured down. Thanks to the canopy over the altar, the pope was protected. The rest of us were drenched, though. Those who had brought umbrellas raised them. Those with raincoats or pieces of plastic held them over their heads. Some who came without any protection from the rain got up and left. Kathy and I and the rest of the volunteers went around to the people with handicaps and asked them if they wanted us to help them get out of the bad weather.

"Are you kidding?" a fairly young guy said to me when I asked him if he wanted to go. "This is the best thing that's ever happened to me."

"I'm staying right here," an older women told me when I asked her. "Why would I ever want to leave?"

None of them wanted to leave, and when I thought about it, it made perfect sense. After all these people had been through, what was a little rain? Handicapped or not, they had gotten this close to God's representative on earth—and they weren't about to give it up. When it came time for communion, as soaked as they were, they all proudly displayed the blue ticket that allowed them the privilege of receiving the Eucharist from the Holy Father. He moved among them carefully, tenderly. They received the Host from him with eyes closed and tears and rain streaming down their faces.

After the Mass was over and the pope had gone, there still seemed to be a special glow, a special feeling, over all of us. We were all soaked through, but happy—even though we still had a lot of work to do. The rain had turned Boston Common into a quagmire, and the tires of the heavy, battery-powered wheelchairs were sunk in the mud. We couldn't roll the chairs, so we had to lift them, almost carry them, from the front of the stage to the street where the vans and buses were waiting. But nobody complained. It had been a great day for all of us, a great way to welcome John Paul II to Boston and America.

4

KEEPING TRACK OF HIM

Following his exploits and growing in admiration

I really began to keep track of John Paul II after that. I followed the rest of his 1979 trip to the United States on television and in the newspapers and news magazines.

From Boston, he went to New York and took the Big Apple by storm, not just with his message but with his sense of humor. When Ed Koch introduced himself as the mayor of New York, the pope told him, "I shall try to be a good citizen."

He hammed it up before twenty thousand adoring young people who packed Madison Square Garden to see him. After they chanted "John Paul II. We love you," the pope, grabbing the microphone like a rock and roll singer, changed back: "Whoo whoo whoo! John Paul loves you, too!" At Yankee Stadium, he reminded a standing-room-only crowd: "We must find a simple way of living. . . . It is not right that the standard of living of rich countries should . . . maintain itself by drawing off . . . the reserves of energy and raw materials that are meant to serve the whole of humanity." For somebody like me, who had been "turned on" to Catholic social teaching by studying what's been called the "great charter of Catholic social doctrine"—Pope Leo XIII's 1891 encyclical *Rerum Novarum*—at Providence College, this was music to my ears.

The music continued when John Paul II addressed the General Assembly of the United Nations where he repeated what Pope Paul VI had said in his appearance at the U.N. in 1965: "No more war—war never again." But popes always spoke out for peace. Speaking out for peace was easy, especially in the United States. Speaking out for justice was harder. But he did that, too. Not only did he call for guaranteeing human rights to all people, he went so far as to list what those rights should be, among them "the right to life, liberty, and security of person; the right to food, clothing, housing, sufficient health care, rest, and leisure; the right to freedom of expression, education, and culture . . . the right to choose a state of life, to found a family, and to enjoy conditions necessary for family life; the right to property and work, to adequate working conditions and a just wage; the right of assembly and association; the right to freedom of movement, to internal and external migration . . . and the right to political participation."

For somebody like me, who was moving up the ladder in politics, but was running into criticism for being "too conservative" because of my opposition to abortion and "too liberal" because I wanted to spend more for affordable housing, education, and health care, this pope was showing me there was no contradiction, that being politically "right" or "left" had nothing to do with being morally and spiritually correct.

And I wasn't the only one who thought so. In Washington, D.C., John Paul had his first meeting with President Jimmy Carter, one of the most religious and moral presidents we have ever had. After spending more than an hour together, the two men went out to the White House lawn to deliver their prepared remarks before the media and a gathering of several thousand people, but President Carter abandoned his speech and just showered praise on John Paul II in what *Time* magazine called "one of the most moving moments of his presidency." Years later, I asked President Carter what that first meeting with John Paul II had been like. "It was incredible . . . incredible," he told me. "The man just radiated a holiness, a kind of glow, that swept you up into it and had you talking from the heart instead of the head. I've never seen anything like it in my life."

Nobody had seen anything like this pope, either in the United States or around the world. A few months later, labor disputes began to break out in Poland, culminating in the strike by workers at the Gdansk shipyard. Taking the "worker-priest" movement to the highest level, they plastered huge pictures of John Paul II over the gates and the walls of the shipyard. And John Paul II backed them up. In speech after speech, he used the word solidarity over and over again. And when the government finally backed down and gave in to the workers' demands, the leader of the striking workers, a till-then unknown electrician named Lech Walesa, used a pen with a picture of John Paul II on it to sign the agreement. Watching all of this from the United States, my admiration for the Holy Father grew even stronger. This was my kind of pope: a pope of the people, a workers' pope, a pope who wasn't afraid to put everything on the line.

5

THE DAY THE POPE WAS SHOT

Somehow everyone understood how much he meant

That's what made the next big news involving John Paul II so hard to hear.

In the spring of 1981, I was asked by a friend, Professor Bob Krim, to serve as guest lecturer in his political science course at Roxbury Community College. The school, like the neighborhood it was in, was struggling. Classrooms and offices were housed in a complex of run-down brick buildings in an area of the city that had still not recovered from the race riots Boston experienced in the 1960s. The school's mission was to serve "nontraditional" students, mostly minority and older students who were trying to upgrade their skills so they could get jobs that would move them a little higher on the economic ladder.

The students in the class I was teaching were all black, mostly men, and mostly criminal justice majors. A lot of them were Vietnam veterans. Some of them were jail or prison guards. Quite a few were Boston police officers. I enjoyed teaching them because they were serious and curious, and they cared about the city and the problems faced by people living in its neighborhoods. One morning in May 1981, I found out they cared about other things as well.

Just after I started teaching that day, one of the students, a Boston police officer named Bruce Halloway, came into the classroom a little bit late. But instead of taking a seat in the back, he walked up to the front of the classroom and paused next to the first row of desks as if he had something to say. I asked him what was going on. I thought maybe somebody's car was blocking a driveway or something.

"Excuse me, Mr. Flynn . . ." he said, not finishing his sentence.

"What is it, Bruce?" I asked him again.

"Well," he said, "it's just that I think you should know . . . I think maybe the rest of the class should know." He had a pained look on his face; clearly he had bad news to deliver.

"Know what?" I asked.

"Well . . . well . . ." he said, first looking down at the floor and then looking up, and directly at me. "It's about the pope. Somebody shot him."

After he said it, things seemed to move in slow motion for me. Everyone talks about being able to remember where they were when President Kennedy was shot. Well, I remember vividly where I was when I found out John Paul II had been shot—and not just because of how I got the news but because of what happened next.

The classroom fell completely silent. Everyone stopped talking, stopped shuffling their papers. All heads were bowed, as if in prayer—either out of respect for the Holy Father or for me, because they knew I was a devout Catholic. The image I still remember is of row after row of heads bowed, of brown eyes in black faces looking down at the floor. I didn't know how many of the students were Catholic; very few, I would have thought. Most of the black residents of Boston that I knew were Protestant, many of them Baptists. I knew some had converted to Islam. But it didn't seem to matter what faith they held; all of them shared in the grief now. It was if, by their silence, they were saying: "If this has happened to you, it's happened to us, too."

No one knew what to do or say. Halloway stood there for a second, then muttered, "I'm sorry," and went and took a seat in the back. The rest of the class remained seated and looking down. What made it even more meaningful to me was that these weren't young, naive, or idealistic college kids. These were people who had seen war and suffering in other countries, seen poverty, murders, rapes, and child abuse on the streets of Boston. Yet here they were, sensitively showing their respect.

The silence lasted for quite a while. It was as if they were saying "We don't know what to do or say. What do Catholics do in situations like this?" They didn't get any clues from me. I was all choked up. I couldn't believe it. It probably seems callous to say now, but I thought: okay, I can understand people trying to assassinate a politician. I can imagine a lunatic shooting Lincoln or JFK. But a religious leader? The pope? This pope? Why this pope? After all he's done in such a short time . . . After all he's trying to do. . . .

My mind was racing. My emotions were churning. There was no way I could continue the class. There was no way I was going to say, "Okay, now let's turn to page 123 in your textbooks and we'll talk about the legislative process." Luckily for me and the students, the real teacher, Bob Krim, came into the classroom then. Bob added another dimension to the sociology of our group, a Jewish intellectual from New York. Judging by the look on his face, I could tell he'd heard the news. He looked first at me, then at all the students, then, very somberly, he spoke. "I guess we've all heard," he said. "I think—given the circumstances—we should probably just suspend the class for today. But before we go . . . maybe we could . . . regardless of our religion . . . have a moment of silence . . . and of prayer . . . for the pope . . . for John Paul II, a man who in such a short time has touched so many people around the world."

If it had been quiet before, it was even more still and silent now. I was standing with my head bowed next to a podium at the front of the room. Bob was next to me. The students were seated. The only thing that broke the silence was an occasional sigh or a sob. This wasn't one of those phony moments of silence they have before a baseball game at Fenway Park. This one was from the heart and felt like it could have gone on forever.

Finally, I gathered myself together and spoke up. If I didn't, we'd have all sat there forever, that's how deeply respectful everyone was being. "Thank you," I said. "Thank you, everybody, for your sensitivity and respect. Let's hope and pray for the best." Then, and only then, did people start to move. They gathered their books and bags, stood up, and slowly left the classroom.

The pope recovered, thank God. If he hadn't, who knows how history might have been changed. People always wonder what might have happened if FDR had not survived the assassination attempt on his life, if Churchill had been hit by a car crossing the street, if JFK had lived. I'm thankful that we don't have to ask ourselves a similar question about John Paul II. I'm also thankful for having been able to experience that moment at Roxbury Community College when people of different races, different backgrounds, and different religions instinctively and immediately came together and showed their respect for the Holy Father, showed their understanding and appreciation of what he meant to the world.

Almost fifteen years later, I told the story of that day to John Paul II. We were sitting together in his cabin in the TWA jet that was taking him back to Rome after his very successful visit to the United States in October 1995. I told him the story because I wanted him to know how much the people of the United States loved and respected him—and had from the first day he ascended to the throne of St. Peter. The Holy Father sat across from me in one of the two chairs of the cabin. As I talked, he leaned forward, his head in his hands, his eyes closed. When I finished the story, he opened his eyes, looked into mine, and said: "That was the day Our Lady saved my life."

6

THREE MEETINGS IN ROME

"We're going to Mass with the pope."

My next opportunity to meet John Paul II came in May 1985, when Boston's archbishop, Bernard Law, was elevated to the rank of cardinal. By then I had been elected mayor of Boston, and so I led the city's delegation that attended the consistory in Rome. It was the first trip to the Eternal City for my wife, Kathy, and me, so just being in Rome was a thrill. But on our second night in the city, it got even better. We were staying at Villa Taverna, the residence of the American ambassador to Italy, at the time Max Rabb, when I received a phone call from a friend who had also made the trip over from Boston, Monsignor Stanislaw Sypek, the pastor of St. Adalbert's, the church in Boston where I'd first met Cardinal Wojtyla back in 1969.

"Can you and Kathy meet me in front of St. Peter's at six o'clock tomorrow morning?" Monsignor Sypek asked over the phone.

"Sure," I replied. "But why?"

"We're going to Mass with the pope," he answered. He hung up before I could ask any more questions. I knew that Monsignor Sypek knew the pope, even though he rarely talked about the Holy Father, both out of his own sense of humility and because of his desire to protect the pope's privacy. But I didn't know how well they were acquainted until the next morning.

Kathy and I were out in front of St. Peter's bright and early, with only the pigeons and Rome's street sweepers to keep us company. Soon, Monsignor Sypek appeared. He's a big, solid-looking guy who looks a lot like the Holy Father. Monsignor Sypek greeted Kathy and me and led us through the colonnade on the right-hand side of St. Peter's to the *Portone di Bronzo*—the "bronze doors"—of the Apostolic Palace. A Swiss Guard stepped forward to meet us. After Monsignor Sypek said something to him in Italian, he let us pass. We followed the monsignor inside the Apostolic Palace, up the long flight of steps of the *Scala Clementina*, took the elevator to the third floor and walked down a long marble corridor. Kathy and I stared at the high vaulted ceilings, the ancient tapestries, and the frescoed maps on the walls. We were both kind of awestruck at *where* we were—and even more at *who* we were going to see.

At the door of the papal apartment, another Swiss Guard approached us. After a few words from Monsignor Sypek, we were shown into the pope's private library. It was a large, bright, high-ceilinged room furnished with dark wood tables and chairs, and bookcases that were filled with a collection of ancient Bibles and what looked to be a complete set of the encyclicals of all the popes. On one wall was a painting of the resurrection of Christ. On another, on either side of a desk, were two wooden carvings.

After we had a few minutes in the library, a nun appeared and led us into the pope's private chapel. I was surprised at how modern it looked; it was a long narrow room with tan walls and lit by a stained-glass ceiling. Up front, the small altar was decorated with ornate gold grillwork on the front. Behind the altar was a curved red marble wall. Mounted on the wall was a large, gold, modernist crucifix. Just to the right of the crucifix hung a small painting of Poland's patron saint, the Black Madonna, Our Lady of Czestochowa.

A few rows of chairs with kneelers in front of them were set out in the chapel. We went over and knelt down, made the sign of the cross and began to pray. Up near the altar, only a few feet away, was another kneeler—or *prie-dieu*, as they're called. At first, I thought some vestments were piled on it, but then the vestments moved and I saw it was John Paul himself. He had been praying so intently, bent so far over the kneeler, that I hadn't noticed him when we first came in. Now, he raised his head for a second, brought his elbows up to the top surface of the kneeler, and pressed his face in his hands, still praying. I remembered him as a fairly big, solidly built man. But now, praying, he seemed small. His whole body seemed to be compressed, concentrated. It was almost like he was in pain, that's how intense he was as he prayed. It was as if he were trying to take away some of Christ's pain, as if he were trying to carry the cross himself. It was exhausting to watch him, and almost a relief when, after five or ten minutes, he made the sign of the cross, straightened up, and rose from the kneeler and stepped to the altar to say Mass.

Two of the Polish nuns from the papal household staff came out and placed cruets of wine and water and a magnificent gold chalice on the altar, then they took their places behind us in the chapel. The pope's private secretary, Monsignor Stanislaw Dziwisz, came in to assist the Holy Father with the service. The mass itself was beautiful and simple. The Holy Father said it in Polish; his baritone voice was strong, his movements around the altar graceful and deliberate, whether handling the cruets of wine and water, wiping the rim of the chalice, or elevating the Host. Just as he had done at Boston Common, he appeared to be offering up his movements as well as his words to God. When it was time for Holy Communion, the pope stepped around from the altar and came forward to us and put the Host on our tongues. Talking about it afterward, both Kathy and I found we had been thinking the same thing—if only our parents, all of whom had been devout Catholics, had been alive to see us receiving the body and blood of Christ from the Vicar of Christ on Earth.

After finishing the Mass in Polish, the pope said, in English: "The Mass is over, go in peace." We continued to kneel as he walked past us and out of the chapel to change out of his vestments. After he was gone we left our seats, and Monsignor Sypek led us back into the library. A few minutes later, the pope came in, dressed simply in his white caped cassock and skullcap. He immediately went over and embraced Monsignor Sypek, then both of them, smiling and laughing, began talking, excitedly and at the same time, in Polish. It was clear they were old friends who hadn't seen each other in a long time. They kept laughing and joking, and then, at the same time, they seemed to remember that they weren't alone and became more serious. Monsignor Sypek brought the Holy Father over to us. We bowed and kissed his ring.

"Visitors from Boston. You are welcome, very welcome," the pope said to us.

Monsignor Sypek introduced me as the mayor of Boston and Kathy as my wife. Usually, when we were introduced that way, I'd get most of the attention. But after welcoming us both and shaking hands with me, the pope devoted all of his attention to Kathy. "Ah, Mrs.," he said. "Your husband has a very important job. Like the pope does. But don't believe it. Your job is more important. The future of the world is with the mothers. It is the mothers who raise the children. It is the mothers who will give us peace and make us free. Like Mary, the Mother of Jesus, we need you the most."

Monsignor Sypek and I just stood there, watching. Kathy was the star of the show. Years later, I'd learn to expect this from the Holy Father. Invariably, he would give most of his attention to those accustomed to getting the least attention. I'd learn how important mothers, in general, and the Virgin Mary, in particular, were to him. I'd discover that when he was in high school he'd started a Marian sodality in his town, that when he became pope he added the letter *M* to his papal coat of arms in honor of Mary, and that he'd written an encyclical, *Redemptoris Mater* (Mother of the Redeemer), in which he placed Mary first, ahead of Peter and the rest of the disciples, in the "long line of witnesses to the Lord." I'd also learn—I'd be told by him personally, actually—that he believed the Virgin Mary saved him from an assassin's bullet. But that was all to come. Right now I was experiencing it all for the first time, as he talked about the importance of women, of mothers, and of Mary to my wife, in his home, inside the Vatican.

The next day, Kathy and I saw the Holy Father again at a special audience for the parishioners of the new cardinals from Boston and New York in Paul VI Hall, an enormous auditorium, just inside the walls of the Vatican, that holds six thousand people. Row after row of seats sweep down from the back of the hall to the bottom, where a shallow stage rises in front of a curtain. The ceiling of the hall is a vaulted, silver-ribbed, glass skylight. Huge, oval stained-glass windows illuminate each wall.

The place was packed, with the Boston and New York delegations seated down front on either side of the middle aisle. After a series of short prayers, the Holy Father descended from the stage to greet the leaders of each of the delegations. Accompanied by Archbishop O'Connor, he went first to the New York side and greeted Matilda Cuomo, wife of then-governor Mario Cuomo, New York City mayor Ed Koch, and the rest of the leaders of the delegation. Then Archbishop Law met him at the middle aisle and brought him over to meet all of us. Archbishop Law first introduced his mother and some other members of his family to the Holy Father. Then he presented the rest of the members of the Boston delegation, starting with Kathy and me.

"Holy Father," Archbishop Law started to say, "these are friends of mine—"

But the pope interrupted him. "Friends of mine, too," he said. "The mayor of Boston and his lovely wife." And he came over and shook our hands.

Archbishop Law looked at the Holy Father and then at Kathy and me. He seemed puzzled.

"They came to Mass with me yesterday," the pope explained. Then, turning to the archbishop and holding his hand out toward Kathy, he said, "And this woman is a great friend of our Blessed Mother."

The next day, Saturday, the Holy Father presided over the elevation of new cardinals on the steps of St. Peter's Basilica. It was the first outdoor consistory in recent memory, held outside to accommodate the large number of cardinals—twenty-eight—and the sizable delegations from dioceses all around the world. Our seats were in the first row of the folding chairs set up on the *sagrato,* the carpeted temporary stage erected on the steps of St. Peter's. From there, we were able to see and hear every detail of the ceremony.

In his homily, which he delivered from a throne set on the top step of St. Peter's—and which we read in translation—the pope called on the new cardinals to "go out to their brethren 'with the wisdom of serpents and the innocence of doves' " (Matthew 10:16). And he reminded them of Christ's exhorting the Apostles to "fear not," to "not let themselves be overcome by fear," and "to have no fear" (Matthew

10:26, 28, 31). As a still-new mayor of a diverse city, I was struck by the Holy Father's emphasis of "the mystery of the unity and plurality of the Church." Speaking to the vast audience about this new group of cardinals from all around the world, he said, "The treasures of diverse cultures are brought into this Church of Rome through their persons." His words made me think of the challenges I faced as I tried to bring together people of different races and backgrounds across the city. Meanwhile, the new cardinals were prostrating themselves on the floor of the *sagrato* in front of the pope before receiving the red hat, or biretta. Afterward, they greeted each of their new fellow members of the college of cardinals. The moment was especially meaningful for the pope because one of the new cardinals was his good friend Archbishop Andrzej Maria Deskur, who had suffered a stroke a few days before the pope's election in 1979.

After the ceremony, the Holy Father came over to greet the leaders of the delegations representing the dioceses of the new cardinals. He seemed extremely happy, smiling and waving to everyone. When he came over to Kathy and me, he smiled and squeezed our hands.

"Thank you for giving Cardinal Law to Boston," I said to the Holy Father.

"Do not thank me," the pope said, smiling. "Just be good to him."

After he finished making the rounds of the various delegations, the pope began to greet some of the other people seated on the stage. I was watching him make his way along the front row of seats, thinking how fit and robust he looked, especially for someone who had survived an almost-fatal gunshot wound. As I watched him work the crowd, out of the corner of my eye I spotted a familiar figure waiting for the pope to approach, a very small woman dressed in the blue-and-white habit of a nun—Mother Teresa.

They were both only a few yards away, and I couldn't make up my mind which one to watch. I decided to focus on the pope, and watched as he continued to make his way along the line, greeting people, shaking hands, giving his blessing—with a string of photographers following along in his wake snapping pictures. Just before he got to Mother Teresa, though, he paused . . . then looked behind him at the photographers . . . and he nodded to them. I couldn't be sure, but it seemed to me that he was waiting for the photographers and cameramen, signaling them to catch up with him, directing them to go ahead of him so they could get a better camera angle for the shot that was coming up. And that's just what they did—all the photographers and TV people kind of leapfrogged past the pope so that when he did resume his course, and came to Mother Teresa, they were in position to capture the moment when these two giants of the Church embraced.

Please understand what I'm trying to say here. I don't mean to imply that the pope was anything less than genuine in his greeting of this woman we all knew was a living saint. The look on his face—the broad smile, the warm eyes, and the way he embraced the little Albanian nun—showed how much he respected, even revered, her. But as a politician, I think I saw John Paul II demonstrating how well he understood the importance of using powerful images to communicate with the world. And he succeeded! That night the picture of Mother Teresa and the pope together appeared on Italian television stations. The next day, the photo ran in all the local and international newspapers all over the world. I had witnessed a real pro in action.

7

BEING OFFERED THE JOB

A chance to represent my country to my church

Eight busy years passed by. John Paul II continued to be the most dynamic, accessible, and outspoken pope of this century. He reached out to the Jewish people, becoming the first pope to visit the Great Synagogue of Rome. He returned to Poland for two more triumphal visits and, not coincidentally, saw Solidarity recognized and communism fall. He stepped up his criticism of materialism and the growing gap between the rich and the poor. He spoke out for human rights and against war, including the Persian Gulf War. Back in the United States, I followed his actions and read his words closely. During that time I was re-elected twice as mayor of Boston and campaigned to help elect Bill Clinton the first Democratic president in twelve years.

In March 1993, on the day before St. Patrick's Day, I received a phone call from President Clinton. He wanted to know if I would serve as United States Ambassador to the Vatican. I hesitated before accepting the job for several reasons. For one thing, I already *had* the job I had always wanted—mayor of Boston. For another, I wasn't sure I wanted to give up the world of local, state, and national politics that I had come to know pretty well after twenty-five years in the business. Did I really want to start from scratch and learn the whole new world of diplomacy and international politics? A third reason was that I didn't know how my family would feel about leaving home and Boston and living in Rome for the next few years.

In the end, though, I found more reasons for taking the job than for passing up the opportunity. One was that it was an honor to be asked to represent my country to the government of my church. Another was because it *was* a challenge. A third was because my wife and kids were all for it. They thought—correctly, as it turned out—that this new job would give us *more* time together than the twenty-four-hour-a-day demands of being mayor of a big city. A fourth reason I took the job was that it would have made my mother and father very proud. They never really approved of my first two career choices— playing professional basketball and getting into politics. But they were devout Catholics, and I knew the job of Ambassador to the Vatican would have their blessing.

The final reason I accepted the appointment was because it would allow me the opportunity to get to know John Paul II, this man I had become fascinated with from a distance. It would give me a chance to see him in action up close and in person.

8

PRESENTING MY CREDENTIALS

My first official meeting—and seeing more sides of the man

In July 1993, after having been confirmed by the U.S. Senate in Washington, D.C. and after spending only a few weeks in Rome, I presented my credentials to John Paul II, to be accepted by him as United States Ambassador to the Holy See. Normally, a new ambassador can wait months before getting the chance to meet with the pope. The reason for the exception in my case was that the Holy Father was traveling to the United States soon for World Youth Day in Denver, Colorado. Before I could take part in the trip I had to be officially accepted as the U.S. envoy to the Holy See.

Since it was July, the pope was staying at Castel Gandolfo, his summer residence, which is located a half hour's drive outside of Rome. On the morning of the ceremony, two *Gentiluomini del Santo Padre* (papal gentlemen-in-waiting) came to the ambassador's residence, Villa Richardson, on Rome's Janiculum Hill, to escort me to my meeting. One of the *gentiluomini* was Joe Hagen, at the time the president of Assumption College in Worcester, Massachusetts. The other was a nephew of Pope Pius XII. Both of them wore white tie and tails. I did, too, but only after struggling to get into the starched dress shirt, needing help from Kathy to fasten the white bow tie, strapping the white cummerbund around my waist, and climbing into the long tailcoat.

As I walked down the spiral staircase to the foyer, where Kathy and the kids were waiting for me, I thought I looked pretty good—until one of my daughters brought me down to earth by saying, "Hey, look at Dad in the monkey suit." Joining them, I saw that Kathy and the girls looked beautiful. Kathy wore a long black lace dress with a veil, and the girls wore angle-length skirts with white buttoned-up-to-the-neck blouses with waist-length sleeves. We were ready to go, I thought, except for one slight problem.

Even though we had only been in Rome for a few weeks, we had already begun to receive guests, relatives, and friends from Boston who stayed with us at our residence. Ginny Tomassini Lane, a close friend of the family, was staying with us at the moment. Ginny was the mother of three boys, a Boston public school teacher, and a devout Catholic. Knowing how much it would mean to her if she could meet the pope, I'd promised to see if I could "sneak her in" with us today. Now, Ginny came down the stairs, wearing a black silk dress, a mantilla over her head, and a nervous expression on her face.

"Ray," she said, "are you sure this is okay? I don't want to get you in trouble or do anything that's not proper."

"It's fine, Ginny," I replied confidently. "The pope loves to meet people. The more the merrier. Don't worry." I didn't tell Ginny that it wasn't the pope I was worried about—it was some of the staff at the State Department and Vatican who were apt to put protocol ahead of people. At that very moment, Mirella Giacolone, secretary for protocol at the U.S. Embassy to the Holy See, was waiting for us in the "Nancy Reagan Sun Room"—named in honor of the former first lady by a previous Republican ambassador who had the addition built before a visit by the president and his wife.

Mirella was going to give us a last minute inspection before we left for Castel Gandalfo. I grew to love Mirella and appreciate the great job she did for the embassy, but that morning I played a little trick on her.

"Julie," I said to my oldest daughter, "why don't you and Ginny go wait in the car. And let Ginny sit next to the window on the outside, and you push way over next to her, okay?" Julie gave me a kind of perplexed look, but, like all of my kids, she was used to this kind of intrigue from growing up in Boston politics and having to do things like dodge the sometimes unfriendly local media.

Once Julie and Ginny went out, the rest of us proceeded into the sunroom. "Julie's not feeling well," I told Mirella. "She's waiting in the car." After seeing that we were dressed appropriately to meet the Holy Father, Mirella walked to the front door of the ambassador's residence with us, as I knew she would. Julie was just visible in the back seat of the big black Cadillac. Ginny was out of sight.

There were five cars in the motorcade that pulled away from the curb outside the residence. In the first car were the *carabinieri,* uniformed federal soldiers who used their car's siren, flashing lights, and the "lollipop" stop signs that the guard riding in the front passenger seat held out the window to force cars ahead of us to pull over and let us go by. The second car was the one in which my escorts and I rode. A third car, carrying three *escortas,* anti-terrorist police armed with machine guns, followed behind us. My wife, Kathy, and four daughters and Ginny rode in the next car. A final car of uniformed Rome *polizia* brought up the rear.

The weather was perfect. It was a beautiful day, not a cloud in the sky. On the highway outside of Rome, we passed the little towns made up of stucco houses with red tile roofs clustered around churches and perched up on hills. The churches were obviously the centers of the community. They reminded me of South Boston, where three-deckers and small two-family houses surrounded the many parish churches.

After half an hour, we drove up the winding road into Castel Gandolfo, a small tourist town high up in the Albano hills. The village consisted mostly of a main street, full of souvenir shops and restaurants, that led into a square, *Piazza Giuseppe Mazzini,* flanked by cafés and with a fountain in the center. With sirens shrieking to clear the traffic and the U.S. and Vatican flags flying from masts on the hoods of the cars, we drew the attention of everyone on the street. Tourists and townspeople alike stopped what they were doing and followed us along the sidewalks. I felt like General Mark Clark liberating Italy as our fleet drove into the square.

I had expected the pope's residence to be outside of town, but there it was, right in the center of things, a large villa that closed off one end of the town square. From the outside, it wasn't that imposing a structure—a rounded stucco, tile-roofed building, four or five stories high, two stories taller than its neighbors. Facing the square was a large wooden gate. Joe Hagen told me that on Wednesdays and Sundays in the summer the pope goes out onto the balcony to bless the crowds that gather in the square below.

As we pulled up to the residence, the tall wooden gate swung open and the cars pulled through it and into an interior courtyard. The limousine I was riding in stopped at the foot of a long flight of stairs that led up to the main entrance of the villa. The two *gentiluomini* got out of the car and stood on either side of me as I got out. At a call of *"Attenzione!"* from their commander, the Swiss Guards in their colorful orange, black, and red striped uniforms held out one arm, extending their halberds, six-foot pikes, and held out their other hands in front of them in a horizontal salute.

An Italian priest who spoke perfect English stepped forward and introduced me to Monsignor Dino Monduzzi, the head of the papal household. I would get to know the monsignor very well and discover that his gruff exterior and impatient manner were affected in order to help make sure that all the Holy Father's events went off like clockwork; underneath it all he had a heart of gold. That day, though, I had to try to outfox Monsignor Monduzzi if I wanted to smuggle in an extra person to meet the pope.

Monsignor Monduzzi and I made small talk, which was difficult because, as it turned out, he didn't speak English any better than I spoke Italian. Meanwhile, Kathy, Ginny, and the four girls got out of their car and joined us. The monsignor shook hands with everyone, then stared down at the little index card he held in his left hand. I can't be sure, but I assumed that it read: "U.S. Ambassador Raymond L. Flynn, his wife Catherine, and four daughters: Julie, Nancy, Katie and Maureen." As he read it, a quizzical look came over his face. Did somebody make a mistake? he was probably thinking. Or maybe, Who is the other woman—too old for a daughter, too young for a mother-in-law? He looked up at us and asked a question—in Italian. But since the rest of the Flynn family's Italian wasn't any better than mine—as yet—the language barrier kept us from explaining, even if we'd wanted to, why there was one more person in our party than there were names on the card!

Monsignor Monduzzi evidently decided not to try to get to the bottom of the mystery. He just shrugged, turned, and led all of us up the stairs into the building. Inside the villa, we followed him down a long corridor. It was like a country version of the Apostolic Palace, the ceilings lined with frescoes, the walls hung with tapestries and paintings. Kathy and I walked side by side, the girls and Ginny trailing behind us, whispering to one another, telling one another to look at this or that. Monsignor Monduzzi brought us into a beautifully appointed room with large windows and a breathtaking view of Lake Albano below. Then he left us alone for a few minutes, probably so that we could gather our thoughts. I was impressed at how everything was timed perfectly, nothing was rushed. We waited expectantly for our meeting with the Holy Father. After a few minutes, Monsignor Monduzzi reappeared in a doorway.

"Ambassador! *Piace conoscerla. Viene con me,*" he said, motioning me to come with him. I nodded a "see you soon" to Kathy, Ginny, and the girls and followed him into another room, even more magnificent than the first. I noticed the telescope set up at a window overlooking the lake, a desk in the far corner with a crucifix set on top of it. It was only then that I saw the pope. He was standing behind the desk, wearing red and gold vestments over a white cassock. The Holy Father smiled, stepped from behind the desk and walked forward to greet me, forcing me to make my first decision as U.S. ambassador to the Holy See.

"When you meet the pope," a State Department functionary had briefed me, "just shake his hand with your right hand and hold your documents in your left. That's what we do for any head of state." The pope and I met in the middle of the room and I instinctively ignored the advice I'd gotten from Foggy Bottom. This wasn't just any head of state, I thought; This was the Vicar of Christ, the successor to St. Peter. I bent and kissed his ring.

"Mr. Ambassador," the pope said, smiling that brimming but tight-lipped smile I would get to know very well over the next several years. Then, displaying either a remarkable memory or the thoroughness of the papal staff's briefing—or both—he said, "From Boston, the mayor of the rain. It is good to see you again." We shook hands, and he put his other hand on top of mine, still smiling that wide, open, beaming smile that immediately puts you at ease. At that moment a door across the room opened and a photographer and a cameraman from *Tele Pace,* the Vatican television station, entered the room accompanied by Monsignor Monduzzi. The pope released my hand and turned slightly to face the cameras. All the details were perfectly choreographed. Boy, these guys are pros, I thought. I handed my papers to the pope, who took them for the benefit of the cameras. Then he handed them to the Monsignor, who, in turn, placed them on the desk.

The photo opportunity part of the meeting was all over in forty seconds. The photographers and Monsignor Monduzzi left the room, and the Holy Father took me by the arm and walked me over to his desk. He touched the back of one of the two chairs, upholstered in red velvet and covered in gold leaf, indicating that I should sit down, walked around and seated himself behind the desk, and placed my papers in the center of the desktop. "How is my friend Cardinal Law?" the pope began. I told the pope that Cardinal Law was well and that he had arranged for me to be welcomed to Rome the previous week by Cardinal Sodano, Archbishop Tauran, Monsignors Jim Harvey and Giovanni Battista Re, and other Vatican officials. "He takes care of his friends from Boston." The pope laughed. "I remember Boston very well," the pope continued. "St. Adalbert's. And Harvard. And the Mass in the middle of the city when it rained so hard. And when you came to Rome when our friend became a cardinal."

I was impressed. The pope had just mentioned all the other times we had met. Now, I'm sure he didn't necessarily remember all those meetings, that he had been reminded of them by his staff. But the easy way that he referred to them put me at ease immediately. The Holy Father asked if my family was settled in Rome and what we had done and seen in the short time we had been there. Then, touching the papers that I had given him and the ones he would give me as part of our exchange, he said, "But we have work to do, yes?"

"The world is very different today," he said, beginning the "work" of our meeting, "not so much divided East and West but divided still by war, by poverty, by a lack of freedom. In Eastern Europe, many countries are being reborn . . . but not easily," he said about the Balkans. "In the Middle East, sometimes we feel there is progress being made. Sometimes we are afraid there is a going back. The future of Lebanon is very troubling to us. Very troubling," he repeated.

"Much pain. Much suffering. People should be able to live in peace and practice their own religion in the Middle East."

When it was my turn to speak, I started with the issue of the Holy See's establishing full diplomatic relations with the state of Israel. I told the pope that both President Clinton and Secretary of State Christopher had brought it up in the last conversations that I had had with them—and so had Cardinal Law of Boston and Cardinal O'Connor of New York. Then I gave him the sales pitch that I had prepared: "We believe that relations between the church and the state of Israel would be good for the peace process, that it would be good for the two great faiths in the United States, and that it would help to further reduce anti-Semitism, both in America and around the world, something that you, Holy Father, have done so much to promote."

The Holy Father shook his head. I didn't know if that meant he was agreeing with me or just that he understood the points I was trying to make. Then he said, "There are other issues, other issues." I wasn't sure what he meant, if he was referring to the details that had to be worked out concerning ownership and use of the holy sites in Israel, or if he was referring to something more general. I'd been briefed beforehand that there seemed to be a split within the *Curia* on the issue, with some of the "old guard" trying to delay the process of engaging in full diplomatic relations with Israel, and with others, including the pope, wanting to go full steam ahead. The pope continued, saying something that completely surprised me: "But in any negotiations, it is always the powerful that must give way to the weak if justice is to be achieved."

I looked at the Holy Father intently. I didn't know if I'd heard him right—or if he'd gotten the phrase, the formula, mixed up. Wasn't it the weak who had to give way to the powerful? That's the way I'd always heard it. But he was looking back at me just as intently. He kind of pursed his lips and shook his head yes, as if to say, "You heard me right, Mr. Ambassador. The strong must give way."

His lesson conveyed, the Holy Father changed the subject. "Talk to me about Ireland and the troubles between North and South. You have experience there. Cardinal Daly has told me that you and Cardinal Law went there together. Are things going in the right way, in the right direction?" I told him that the recent granting of a visa to Sinn

Fein leader Gerry Adams was a sign that the Clinton administration was willing to become more involved in the peace process there. "I hope that is so," he said.

The pope kept going, hitting all the bases, all the trouble spots around the world. "We must not forget Africa," he said. "So many people, so much suffering. It is very complicated, each country. But we must not use that as an excuse not to get involved." I mentioned, as I was instructed to, the Clinton administration's concern about Somalia. The pope continued, his choice of topics and words giving me a glimpse of his view of what the most pressing concerns facing the planet were. He said religious freedom was an issue that was, of course, very important to him and the Church, especially in the Far East. He didn't mention the name of any particular country, but I knew from my briefings in Washington and in Rome that East Timor, Indonesia, Vietnam, and particularly China topped the list.

At one point in our discussion, a door opened and Monsignor Monduzzi appeared in the doorway. I wondered if he had been summoned, if the pope had pressed some kind of button under his desk to signal that he was ready to end our meeting. Apparently that wasn't the case, though, because the pope shook his head as if to say, "It's all right. Leave us alone." The monsignor stepped back out of the room and closed the door, and we continued our discussion.

"Holy Father," I asked at one point, "of all the places on earth, which one troubles you most?"

"Most?" he repeated after me, as if going down a mental list. "I cannot say 'most.' But southern Sudan is very troubling. No rules. No law. Only chaos. Only pain. People suffering . . . dying. Many in Christ's name. Asked to choose between their faith or food for themselves and their families. And many are choosing their faith. Martyrs . . . modern martyrs. But no one knows them." He shook his head and sighed. A look of sadness swept across his face.

In my experience, meetings between "top officials" in the United States rarely produced discussions with any substance. Most of the time, they were set up to say you had the meetings—and agreements and disagreements and next steps were worked out ahead of time by the respective staffs. This was different; this was a serious, heart-to-heart talk about issues that mattered. I wished we could have gone on and on, but I knew that we had covered most of the issues contained in our respective statements and that our time was almost up. But there was one more thing I wanted to say.

"Holy Father, I hope you don't mind, but I would like to tell you this," I said. "When I was a little boy, my parents had a shrine in our house . . . in a corner of the kitchen . . . dedicated to Our Lady of Fatima. And every night, after dinner, we used to gather in front of that shrine to say the rosary along with Cardinal Cushing, who had a radio program at seven o'clock. We prayed to Our Lady of Fatima for the conversion of Russia, for the end of communism, and for peace in the world." John Paul II was watching me intently across the desk as I talked. "Holy Father," I continued, "I just want to say that I feel that I am with the one person in the world who is most responsible for making those prophecies come true."

John Paul's face was serious, but then just the trace of a smile came across it. "Mr. Ambassador," he finally said, "perhaps it is more that Our Lady answered your family's prayers." It was an amazing display of graciousness and humility from this man of God, but he didn't stop there. "Many more have their freedom today—as you in the United States have had it for so long," he said. "But we need more than freedom. Freedom should not be wasted. Freedom needs and demands truth . . . it needs responsibility, the responsibility for what is right, for the sanctity of human life and dignity."

Wow, I thought to myself. What an amazing way he has about him, what an amazing manner and mind! First, he accepts my compliments for what he's done so graciously. But then, gently but firmly, he lets me know that there's still plenty of work to do—especially in the country that I had come to The Vatican to represent.

The door behind me opened again. This time the pope stood up, a signal that our meeting was over. Smiling, he came around from behind his desk. "I am looking forward to seeing your wife again—and meeting your daughters." I stood up, he took my arm, and we started back across the room. Just as we reached the middle of the room—as if on cue—the other door opened and Kathy, Ginny, and the girls were shown in.

The pope greeted Kathy. She bent and kissed his ring, and when she stood back up he hugged her as if they were old pals. "I remem-

ber you," the Holy Father said, "with my friend Monsignor Sypek."
Kathy beamed, and I was impressed once again at what a great memory the pope had and/or how well briefed he was on everything. I
wondered if he even knew about the controversy Kathy had gotten
into back in Boston after I accepted the ambassador's job—when she
told a reporter that she was "looking forward to my husband going to
Rome to work for the pope." The newspapers and TV stations played
it up big in Boston—and people at the State Department hit the roof.
Our good friend, Cardinal Law, loved it, though. He teased Kathy
about it every time he saw her. I wondered if maybe he had even told
the pope about it, but the Holy Father didn't mention it.

The pope asked Kathy how she liked Rome and said that he was
looking forward to meeting our two sons ". . . but now I want to
meet your lovely daughters."

Before that could happen, I stepped forward and introduced our
"extra guest." "Holy Father, this is Mrs. Lane, She is a very close
friend of our family and her children attend St. Mary's Polish school
in South Boston."

As I had expected, the pope easily accepted Ginny's presence and
beamed at the mention of the "Polish school." He stepped forward,
took Ginny's hand, and said, "Welcome" and "Remember me to the
children in your school."

Now it was time for the Holy Father to meet the Flynn girls, and
they all lined up to kiss his ring according to age, youngest first—
Maureen . . . Katie . . . Nancy. Julie was last. Before she stepped forward, I told the pope that, six years before, Julie and I had gone to
New Orleans to greet him on his last visit to the United States. "We
waited for hours, first in the hot sun and then in the pouring rain.
And then you came. But just as you came to where we were standing,"
I told the Holy Father, "Julie got so excited she fainted. I had to catch
her before she hit the ground."

The pope listened to my story. Then he looked at Julie very seriously. In a very stern voice, he said to her, "I will bless you now,
then—but only if you promise not to faint." We all laughed, including the pope—*especially* the pope, who, I would learn, invariably gets
a big kick out of his own jokes. Even Julie laughed, although she
turned red with embarrassment.

The photographer came back into the room then and took some more pictures. The next day, one of those photographs appeared in a Boston newspaper above a caption listing John Paul II, the Flynn family, and "an unidentified family friend." As we were posing for the pictures, I couldn't get over all the different "sides" of himself that the pope had just shown in less than an hour's time. Generosity. A keen grasp of the issues. Preparation and attention to detail. Humility. A no-nonsense toughness. Graciousness in welcoming an unexpected guest. And a sense of humor that put our family at ease and drew us close to him. I knew right then that I had done the right thing in taking this job, and I looked forward to seeing more of this man and to getting to know him better.

9

WORLD YOUTH DAY, DENVER

Rocky Mountain high

Pope John Paul II's trip to Denver for the fifth World Youth Day in August 1993 gave me another chance to understand him and a front-row seat from which to experience the joy he generated in America's young people.

In my short time in Rome, I had already heard that some Church officials didn't think it was a good idea for the pope to go to Denver. They were concerned about the kind of reception he might get, afraid that American society was too materialistic and that American young people wouldn't be interested in what he had to say. At Castel Gandolfo, when I presented my credentials as ambassador, the pope himself asked me about young people in America. "You must know them," he said. "You have been mayor of the big city of Boston. You have six children yourself. Tell me. Do they want to see the pope? Will they listen to what he has to say?"

I told him that I thought they would and that American young people were "just like young people everywhere."

"But we read things. We hear such stories . . ." the pope said, not finishing his sentence. I assumed he was talking about the use of drugs and the increase in violence, among young people, about things like MTV and the rest of the "youth culture" in the United States that were now being copied in Europe and around the world.

"The stories and what is on television," I said, "don't reflect most of the young people in America." To illustrate my point, I told him a story about something that happened in Boston when I was mayor, an incident that I thought said a lot about how young people—like a lot of other groups—are not treated fairly by the media.

"There was a shooting in Boston on a Friday night," I told him. "A young person was killed. Another young person was suspected of being his killer. I went to where it happened. There were many TV cameras there, and they were filming the group of young people who gathered on the street as the police and the ambulance came. It was late, and the only young people out at that time were the gang members and hoodlums who were looking for trouble—and those were the young people everyone saw on the television news that night, but"—and here I paused for effect—"they weren't the same young people I saw the next morning."

The Holy Father sat across from me, listening intently. "For some reason," I continued, "I didn't know why, I went back the next morning to the area where the shooting had taken place. There were a lot of young people in the area then as well. But they weren't standing around on the street corner; they were all going into a church. I followed them into the basement of the church. There was a kitchen there, and the young people were fixing meals to take to elderly people, shut-ins who couldn't leave their apartments. But there were no TV cameras showing what these young people were doing."

The pope nodded when I finished my story, and tapped his fingers on the arms of the armchair he was sitting in. "I know you are correct, Mr. Ambassador," the pope said. "The television . . . the newspapers . . . they don't see everything. They don't show everything. I am glad you told that story about America. It gives hope."

I left Rome for Denver a few days before the pope, and stopped first in Washington. Then, on Thursday, August 12, I flew to Denver with President Clinton and his family on *Air Force One*, after a stop in St. Louis to inspect the damage from the recent flooding of the Missouri River. This was going to be the president's first meeting with the pope, and even though I had sent him briefing material—through the State Department—on the pope and the issues that most concerned him, the president seemed a little anxious about the meeting. On the flight to Denver, he asked me a lot of questions. "Does the pope really know all this stuff? Does he go into it to this level of detail?" the president asked, pointing to all the briefing material that was strewn around his cabin. I told him that he did, that he was.

"The Vatican likes to paint a picture of a man of God who is too holy to bother reading newspapers or watching television," I said. "But he's incredibly well read and well informed. He's been everywhere. And he talks to people . . . all the time . . . people from all over the world. He asks questions and he listens. He might not be young anymore, but he's just as sharp, just as up on what's going on as ever." The president listened and nodded, but I wasn't sure he believed me. Then he shifted his line of questioning to what the pope was like personally.

"Is he formal? Will he be relaxed?" The president asked. "Does he talk from notes or just wing it? Does he have a sense of humor? Somebody said he has trouble hearing out of one ear. Which one? Should I make sure to stand on his other side?" I answered every question he asked as well as I could. But from my own experience, I knew that nothing I would tell him could really prepare him for meeting this man.

Air Force One landed at Stapleton Airport in Denver at about one-thirty P.M. We were greeted by Colorado governor Roy Roemer, Denver mayor Wellington Webb, and the rest of the delegation of public officials. There were about a thousand people altogether at the airport as part of the welcoming committee, all gathered in a special area out on the tarmac. While we were waiting for the pope's plane, I introduced the president to a number of U.S. Catholic Church officials, including Cardinals Law of Boston, O'Connor of New York, Bernadin of Chicago, Hickey of Washington, Mahony of Los Angeles, Bevilacqua of Philadelphia, and Krol, the retired archbishop of Philadelphia. I noticed, though, that even as they were shaking hands with the president they were looking past him, out toward the runway, for any sign of the pope's plane. It was very clear who they had come out to see.

At about two-thirty the pope's plane finally arrived. The crowd—Church officials and young people representing the World Youth Day delegates—had given the president polite applause when the doors of

Air Force One opened and he and the First Family came down the steps. But now, when the pope's *Alitalia* plane landed and the Holy Father appeared in the doorway, white-caped, white-capped, and with an expectant look on his face, as if he was curious about how he would be received, the teenagers in the crowd cheered wildly. Then they started chanting "John Paul II. We love you." The pope, standing at the top of the stairs, kind of squinted, then broke into a wide smile.

The pope descended the stairs and proceeded along the red carpet that had been rolled out by U.S. Marines. I stepped forward to meet him, and we walked together to the president, where I introduced the Holy Father to President and Mrs. Clinton and their daughter, Chelsea. They all shook hands, then the pope made his way along the receiving line of American officials, who shook hands with him, and Catholic clergy, who bowed and kissed his ring. The pope, the president, and I walked over to where the two men were to make their brief remarks. "I hope I did not bring the rain," the pope said as we walked. Neither the president nor I knew how to reply, so we didn't say anything. Then the pope looked at me with a mischievous grin. "Maybe the ambassador brought it with him. Maybe he went to Boston first and brought it from Boston." Now, both the president and I laughed. "It doesn't matter," the Holy Father continued, "the rain will wash the mountains. It will make them that much more beautiful for our Mass on Sunday morning."

The program started, but things didn't go very well. The White House advance team was in charge of this event, but they hadn't done a very good job. The podium was out in the open, with no protection against the rain that seemed ready to start falling at any time. When the president started to speak, it turned out that the microphone wasn't working, and he had to shout to make himself heard. Just then, it started to rain, slowly at first, then harder. Someone from the papal advance team stepped from the crowd and went around the small plat- form and held a large, yellow-and-white papal umbrella over the Holy Father to protect him. Nobody did that for the president, though. He was getting drenched, the ink from the notes on his index cards blur- ring, until finally he gave up on using them. Monsignor Robert Tucci, S.J., director of the pope's advance team, and a real stickler for detail and preparation, caught my eye. He was standing a few feet away, and he held up another one of the papal umbrellas, then nod-ded toward the president. I walked over to him, took the umbrella that he offered me, walked behind the president, and held it over him—not exactly my job, but somebody had to do it.

When the president finished speaking, it was the pope's turn. With a papal aide still holding the umbrella over his head, the Holy Father thanked the president, Mrs. Clinton, and Chelsea for welcoming him to America. He asked everyone to pray for the victims of the floods in the Midwest, then he talked about the purpose of his visit. "There is special joy in coming to America for the celebration of this World Youth Day," he said, coming to "a nation which is itself still young—still young. What is two hundred years for a nation?" The crowd laughed and cheered. Turning serious, the pope said, "A nation which is itself still young according to historical standards is hosting young people gathered from all over the world for a serious reflection on the theme of life—the human life, which is God's marvelous gift to each one of us, and the transcendent life which Jesus Christ, our Savior, of-fers those who believe in his name." The crowd responded to his words by cheering again.

"No country, not even the most powerful, can endure if it deprives its own children of this essential good," the pope warned. The crowd cheered again, louder now. Sensing that he had something going with his audience, the pope started playing to the crowd. "You are for what God says, what the pope says?" the pope asked. "Or against?" The crowd chanted "For! For!" The pope smiled and nodded his head yes, as if he was satisfied with their response.

Then, in what for me was one of the best parts of a weekend filled with great speeches, the pope said, "America, you are beautiful. Beautiful, and blessed in so many ways. But your best beauty, your richest blessing, is found in the human person, in each man, woman, and child, in every immigrant, in every native-born son and daughter. The ultimate test of your greatness is the way you treat every human being, but especially the weakest and most defenseless ones. The best traditions of your land presume respect for those who cannot defend themselves."

The next day, the press would play up what the pope said next, when he repeated the same line he had used to end his last visit to the

United States, in 1987: "If you want equal justice for all, and true freedom and lasting peace, then, America, defend life." The next day stories would describe how the president stood "stony-faced"; they played up the moment as a confrontation between the pope and the president over abortion. But by focusing on the negative, the press missed the more significant—and positive—part of the pope's message: the celebration of the gift of life. The crowd at the airport didn't miss it, though. They got it—and cheered every word. And as soon as the pope finished and he and the president came down from the small stage, the people in the audience crowded up against the security barriers and stretched out their hands to touch him. Beaming at the warm reception, John Paul II made his way along the barriers, reaching out, shaking as many hands and touching as many people as he could before he was ushered away to the helicopter that was waiting to take him to the next event, his private meeting with President Clinton.

The meeting took place in Carroll Hall at Denver's Regis University, a Jesuit school in a residential neighborhood just outside the city. I flew out to the school with the president and his family in a U.S. Marine helicopter. Once we got to the campus, I walked with the president to the door of the room where the meeting was to take place, but didn't go in. The meetings between the pope and heads of state are private; they meet alone, unless an interpreter is needed. The meetings can last anywhere from twenty minutes to an hour, depending on how the conversation flows. This meeting lasted for a little over half an hour. After it was over, I was called into the room. The president and the pope were each standing behind their chairs, separated by a small table that held a pitcher of water and two glasses. I tried to get a reading from their body language as to how the meeting had gone, but couldn't. Both of the men seemed formal, neither friendly nor aloof.

As I followed the two men out of the room and over to the outdoor area where they were going to deliver short statements, the president's press secretary, Dee Dee Myers, told me, "We better watch out. They're looking for blood." I knew by "they" she meant the media, and it didn't take long for me to realize that she was right.

While we were walking, a network television reporter caught up to me. "It must have been a wild meeting," she said. "I heard the pope stuck his finger right in the president's face and lectured him about abortion being a sin!" I didn't answer her, so she continued. "And then the president told the pope, 'In the United States, abortion is a political issue, not a religious one.'"

Finally, I couldn't take it anymore. "Where did you get this?" I asked her. I'm sure my voice betrayed my anger and my disbelief.

"From a Polish bishop," she answered. "And it was confirmed by someone in the White House press office." She asked me if *I* would confirm it, and I told her I would do no such thing. "Will *they* confirm it, then?" she asked, pointing just up ahead to the president and the pope. Just then, we arrived at the area where the speaking program was to take place and the reporter left, going around into the crowd of media up front. I caught up to the president and the pope just before they got to the podium.

"Excuse me for asking," I said, "but could any part of your meeting today be described as confrontational?" The president looked at me like he was surprised that I would ask such a direct question. The pope only smiled and shook his head no. "I'm only asking," I said, "because I think that's what the press thinks . . . that it's what they're going to ask."

The president still had a kind of bewildered look on his face. But the pope playfully grabbed my arm and pulled me close to him, saying to President Clinton: "The ambassador, he has some experience with the American media?" Then both of them laughed, I guess at my expense.

But I had to ask the question again. "Well, are you going to answer their questions?"

The pope turned serious. He shook his head no. "I am a Catholic priest," he said. "I do not talk about what people tell me in confidence."

"But if they ask—" I said.

The pope interrupted me. "You will answer any questions," the pope said, and stepped away.

"Me?" I said, mostly to myself.

"Yeah, you," the president said then. "You take the questions after we're gone." With that, he joined the Holy Father at the microphones.

The ceremony was very brief. The president spoke first, calling the meeting "cordial and productive." He listed some issues they discussed, including Somalia, the Sudan, Haiti, and Bosnia, and said, "We believe that we can make progress in dealing with them." When it was the pope's turn, the seventy-three-year-old pontiff had a little fun with the forty-six-year-old president: "I am still and still older and he's still and still younger." The pope went on to say that it was very appropriate to be greeted by such a young president on the occasion of World Youth Day.

When the pope finished speaking, somebody from the White House announced that if members of the press had any questions they should go over to another building, a few hundred yards or so away, where "Ambassador Flynn will be glad to answer your questions." Then the president and the pope went off to their respective helicopters, the president bound for a fund-raising event in California, the pope on the way to his first World Youth Day event, leaving me to deal with the press, my job to do something every politician hates—not make news.

The pope's next stop was at Mile High Stadium, just outside Denver, where a crowd of ninety thousand young people had jammed themselves into the Denver Broncos' football stadium and waited in the rain for hours to see him. Just after six o'clock, with the rain pausing momentarily and lightning still flashing in the sky, the giant electronic scoreboard inside the stadium showed the pope's helicopter landing, and a cheer went up from the crowd. A few minutes later, the pope came into the stadium, riding in the back of the Rocky Mountain version of the "popemobile," a red, flat-topped pickup truck with green-tinted windows. Riding with him were Denver's Archbishop J. Francis Stafford and Eduardo Cardinal Pironia, head of the Pontifical Council for the Laity, which was responsible for putting together the Youth Day event. Trailing behind, on foot, were Vatican security and Secret Service. More security people rode behind in a black limousine.

The crowd started cheering, singing, dancing, waving banners, and screaming. It looked—and sounded—more like a rock concert than a religious event. A huge stage, decorated in green and pink, was set up in front of the south stands. An altar was set up on the stage and had been covered by a canopy. Two tall towers of scaffolding for the sound and light systems stood on either side. The pope got off the temporary popemobile and greeted people as he made his way toward the stage, working the crowd, reaching to shake hands over a chain link fence. This was probably the happiest I'd ever seen the Holy Father. He was smiling, waving, bouncing around, really lit up. Over the years, I would find out that the presence of young people did that to him, for him. He loved to be with them, seemed younger himself when he was with them. When he had to meet political leaders his face would tighten up as if he was getting ready to do something he didn't really enjoy. But when he was with young people I never saw that look. Instead, he was always relaxed, always energized.

After he greeted as many of the young people as he could, the pope climbed up the stairs to the stage. He hugged the young people who had somehow been lucky enough to sit on the stage, then went over and sat down in a kind of thronelike chair while ninety thousand people chanted "John Paul II! We love you!" over and over and over again. I sat with a group of young people from New York who clapped until their hands were red and swollen and who cheered and screamed until their voices were hoarse. I couldn't get over how excited they were—although the next day I read in the newspaper that wasn't the proper description. "Exciting isn't the right word," Jose Maria Elias, a twenty-year-old computer science student from Barcelona told the *Denver Post*. "If you have a father and you only see him a few times a year, you are happy—so happy that when you see him you want to explode. That is how I feel." And that, I guess, is how most of the young people felt.

Archbishop William Keeler of Baltimore, chairman of World Youth Day and president of the National Conference of Catholic Bishops, delivered upbeat welcoming remarks. He talked about how the Catholic Church in the United States added a million Catholics the previous year and how enrollment in Catholic schools and in seminaries was going up. Each of those announcements provoked a cheer from the crowd. Then the pope got up from his chair and approached the podium. He stood in the middle of the stage, under a canopy to protect him from the elements, wearing his white-caped robe and white *zuchetto*, or skullcap. And the place—as Boston Celtics announcer Johnny Most used to say—"went wild." The applause that was only *loud* before was *earsplitting* now. The young people stamped their feet so hard the whole stadium shook. The roaring and shaking kept on for what seemed like ten minutes. Finally, the pope held up his hands like a football quarterback asking for quiet. It was the same thing that John Elway of the Denver Broncos had done so many times in this same stadium. But when Elway had done it, it was so that his football teammates could hear him shout his signals. The Holy Father was doing it now so the young people could hear the word of God.

The pope began preaching. He asked the young people there to open their "minds and hearts to the goodness and beauty of the world around us." He said, "We have come to Denver as pilgrims. Ours is a pilgrimage to a modern city, a symbolic destination. The metropolis is the place which determines the lifestyle and the history of a large part of the human family at the end of the twentieth century." Then he invited the young people "to enter into the depths of your hearts and to live the next few days as a real encounter with Jesus Christ." He continued for forty-five minutes, and I had never been in a place so big, with so many people, that stayed so quiet. Even when, twenty-five minutes into his talk, the rains came again, everyone sat in silence. The next day, the *Denver Post* described the gathering as a "sea of love."

As he was finishing his talk, the Holy Father apologized to the crowd. "My speech was too long, too long," he said, shaking his head and begging their forgiveness. But the crowd shouted "No! No!" They wanted more. They wanted an encore! But the pope, veteran actor that he was, knew when to stop. He closed by saying, "With great joy, I look forward to our next meeting. *Hasta la vista!*"

The next day, Friday, August 13, the pope took it easy—for him, at least. After saying Mass with the members of the U.S. Bishops Conference in Denver's Cathedral of the Immaculate Conception in the morning, he went for a walk in the foothills of the Rockies. There's a great picture of him, wearing the yellow sneakers that the young people gave him as a gift, standing on the shore of a lake, planting a crucifix in the ground with the Rocky Mountains in the background. That night, he returned to Mile High Stadium—another standing ovation from another capacity crowd—for the stations of the cross.

On Saturday, the pope concelebrated a Mass at McNichols Arena for seventeen thousand people. In his homily, he talked about the unacceptable increase in violence in the world, especially in the United States. But the part of his talk that provoked the biggest response from the crowd was his decision to take on the media. Speaking of violence, the Holy Father said, "The question which must be asked is: Who is responsible? Individuals have a responsibility for what is happening. Families have a responsibility. Society has a heavy responsibility. Everybody must be willing to accept their part of this responsibility—including the media." The last remark got the biggest response, and so he said it again. "Including the media, which in part seem to become more aware of the effect they can have on their audiences." The applause was even louder this time—so the pope, knowing a good thing when he found it, kept it up. "I repeat once more: including the media." Then, as his sense of humor caught up with his sense of the dramatic, he poked fun at himself. Gesturing toward the television cameras that were broadcasting his speech, the Holy Father said, "So now the pope is speaking out against the television that presents him." The crowd laughed—and cheered. Then, since he never picks on any one group or institution—even the media—the pope asked the audience, "Who is responsible for the media?" To which they responded, loudly, "We are. We are." The pope turned serious again, though. He denounced a "culture of death" in which "objective goodness and evil no longer . . . matter. Good comes to mean what is pleasing or useful at a particular moment. Evil means what contradicts our subjective wishes." At the end, having used all the tools in his tool belt—a well-prepared text, effective ad-libs, rhetoric to heighten the drama of his speech, humor to lighten things up just a little bit, and strong words to tell hard truths—the pope made the sign of the cross and blessed everyone.

John Paul II was staying at Archbishop Stafford's residence, next to the Cathedral in downtown Denver, and every night, when he got back there, thousands of young people—including young priests and nuns—gathered around the rectory, hoping for the chance to see him. But even though there were large numbers of people, they were all so polite and well-behaved they didn't cause a bit of trouble. Instead, they gathered in small groups to pray or sing songs. Some had guitars, and they would lead sing-alongs to songs like "If I Had a Hammer," "Sing a Song of Freedom," "Prayer of St. Francis," and "We Shall Overcome." They wouldn't sing too loudly. It wasn't a mass concert or anything like that, just small groups, many composed of people with beautiful voices, singing quietly. One night, though, they did all join together to sing the same songs and serenade the Holy Father after he'd gone inside. In a little while, he came out onto the balcony of the rectory. He talked and joked for quite a while, then he told them that it was late and he was tired and they must all go to bed, and he went inside. Just like that, everyone headed back to the hotels or hostels or schools or the church basements where they were staying. But before they did, they picked up after themselves, every candy wrapper or soft drink can. I mentioned this to a guy who worked for the Denver Public Works Department, and he was just as impressed as I was. "These kids are a dream," he said, "a real dream."

People all over Denver got to see just what a dream they were on Saturday, when thousands of young people took part in what was called "The Pilgrimage," a fourteen-mile march from downtown Denver, where most of the events and workshops were held, to Cherry Creek State Park for the all-night prayer vigil that preceded the Sunday morning closing Mass. Somewhere around fifty thousand of them marched, and it was an amazing sight to see them, carrying flags from their schools and churches, singing, praying, and holding hands. These were kids who had given up summer vacations, who had washed cars in church parking lots, whose mothers held bake sales and fathers sold raffle tickets at work just so they would come to see the seventy-three-year-old Bishop of Rome and head of their church. Thousands of residents poured out of their homes and apartment buildings to watch these young people pass by and I'm sure it was a thrill for these Denver families to see that not all young people had lost their values or their faith in God.

At Cherry Creek State Park that night, the crowd was estimated at a quarter of a million people. The next day the papers would describe it as a "Catholic Woodstock." Once again, the pope arrived by helicopter, this time right at sunset. Once again, the young people gave him a tremendous ovation. The pope took his place, sitting in a chair on the stage, and listened to the musical performances that began the program. But the best performances came from the pope and from the crowd. At one point, the audience all began chanting, "*Juan Pablo Segundo. Te ama todo el mundo!* [John Paul II. Everybody loves you]." And the pope replied, "No, no. *Aquí se habla inglés!* (No, no. Here we speak English)." Then, when they did chant in English, the pope answered, "John Paul II. He loves you, too. But Christ, he loves you more!"

The crowd quieted and listened attentively to the pope's homily. I was sitting on the stage, right next to the main altar, so I could observe the whole spectacle of the hundreds of thousands of young people out in the audience, and see the delight on the Holy Father's face as the young people responded so positively to his talk, which was very serious and somber. The pope said, "A 'culture of death' seeks to impose itself on our desire to live and live to the full. There are those who reject the light of life, preferring the 'fruitless works of darkness.' Their harvest is injustice, discrimination, exploitation, deceit, violence. In every age, a measure of their apparent success is the death of innocents. In our own century, as at no other time in history, the 'culture of death' has assumed a social and institutional form of legality to justify the most horrible crimes against humanity: genocide, 'final solutions,' 'ethnic cleansings,' and the massive taking of life of human beings even before they are born or before they reach the natural point of death."

The next day, the media played up the abortion issue and the pope's use of the phrase "culture of death." But, to me, the most memorable line of his speech that night was his instruction to the young people: "Do not give in to the widespread false morality . . . Do not stifle your conscience." The Holy Father was using the positive peer group pressure of an extraordinary, once-in-a-lifetime event that I'm sure these young people would never forget to help them combat any negative peer group pressure they might encounter when they went back to their homes and their daily lives.

Sunday was the absolute highlight of the weekend, though. When John Paul II picked Denver as the site of the World Youth Day event, a lot of people—both inside and outside the church—weren't sure he could pull it off. Denver, Colorado, wasn't a holy city like the previous sites of Youth Day events—Rome, Santiago de Compostela, or Czestochowa. It didn't have the same large numbers of Catholics to draw from like Buenos Aires. The American church was going to do its best, parishes all over the country promised to work hard for a year to organize delegations to send, but even the most optimistic church officials expected only about 50,000 or 60,000 young people to attend. Imagine how pleased they were on Wednesday to find that 200,000 had signed up. Imagine how surprised they were on Saturday night when 250,000 attended the prayer vigil. Imagine how delighted they were on Sunday morning when 375,000 people showed up at Cherry Creek State Park for the papal Mass. As one bishop told me, "We'd all like to think it was the result of all our hard work—but we know there's only one person responsible, and he's sitting up on the stage in that chair."

By Sunday morning, the rain of the previous four days had gone, replaced by a blazing sun. A huge stage, bigger than the one at Mile High Stadium, was set up at one end of an open field. On either side were sets of bleachers for church officials and Youth Day delegates. The altar, in the middle, was carpeted in red and white and covered by a crescent-shaped canopy. Some of the Denver police officers assigned to the event gave me a ride out to the park early Sunday morning, and I spent a few hours just walking around and soaking in the amazing spectacle. There were young people from all over the country, from all over North America, actually—black and white, Hispanic, and Asian. Most of them had been at the park all night. I'm sure none of them had gotten much sleep, but they were all cheerful and full of energy. They were singing songs, saying prayers. Most of them were wearing T-shirts and caps or carrying banners, that identified where they were from. I went looking for groups from New England,

and finally ran into a group of young people from Fall River, Massa-chusetts.

I asked them when they'd arrived in Denver, and they told me Wednesday. I asked them where they were staying and they told me the name of a church I don't remember. "In dormitories?" I asked. "We wish!" one of them yelled from the back, and they all laughed. "No," said a husky kid wearing a Red Sox cap who was standing in the front. "We're in the classrooms. We're sleeping on the floor." I asked them why they had come. "To see the pope!" they all said at the same time. Then, "And the mountains," one of them joked.

"Why do you like the pope so much?" I inquired. "What's so spe-cial about him?"

The group got quiet then, taking my question seriously. The boy in the Red Sox cap spoke up, confidently, not self-consciously, and without looking behind him for approval. "Because we trust him," the young man said. "Because we want someone to believe and we know we can believe him."

"But why?" I persisted. "Just because he's the pope?" I knew I was pressing him, playing the devil's advocate, but playing the devil's ad-vocate for the Holy Father. I wanted to get to the bottom of the spe-cial relationship John Paul II seemed to have with young people around the world.

"No," the young man said earnestly. "Not just because he's the pope, but because he's the kind of pope he is. Because he doesn't just tell us what we want to hear. He tells the truth—even when it's hard for us to hear sometimes. That's how we know we can trust him. That's why we love him so much. That's why we came all this way to see him."

Once again, the sight of the pope's helicopter provoked cheers from the huge crowd. Once again, the cheers grew louder when he came riding into view in the popemobile, and they grew even louder as the little red truck glided down the aisles between the hundreds of thou-sands of standing, jumping, screaming young people. The crowd qui-eted, respectfully, once the pope ascended the stage, until he began the Mass. "In the name of the Father, and of the Son, and of the Holy

Spirit," he intoned, "I say good morning." Then the sea of young people roared "Good morning!" back and cheered again.

The pope proceeded to say the Mass, assisted by Denver's Archbishop Stafford and other priests and with music provided by local church choirs. The Holy Father's homily was another great piece of preaching. He talked about responsibility, his own as well as everyone else's. "Woe to me, woe to me if I do not evangelize," he said. "Woe to you if you do not succeed in defending life." He went on talk about the responsibility to support families. "The family especially is under attack," he warned. "And the sacred character of human life is denied. Naturally, the weakest members of society are the most at risk: the unborn, children, the sick, the handicapped, the old, the poor and unemployed, the immigrant and refugee." I couldn't help thinking—after he said that last line—of something that the late Hubert Humphrey used to say and I used to quote whenever possible: "The moral test of government is how it treats those in the dawn of life—our children; those in the twilight of life—the elderly; and those in the shadows of life—the sick, the needy, and the unemployed."

The pope's sermon that Sunday morning was full of what those of us in politics call "home cookin'" and had more "good lines" than any I had heard him deliver so far. Keeping the pressure on, continuing to challenge the young people, he told them at one point: "Do not be afraid to go out on the streets and into public places like the first apostles who preached Christ and the good news of salvation in the squares of cities, towns, and villages. This is no time to be ashamed of the Gospel. . . . It is the time to preach it from the rooftops."

I've been at a lot of political rallies. The best was the election eve rally in Boston Garden for John F. Kennedy in 1960. Another good one was the 1984 Democratic Party National Convention in San Francisco that featured Mario Cuomo's rousing speech reminding everybody what the Democratic Party was supposed to stand for. But the pope's speech this Sunday morning topped them all, as far as I was concerned. Where other speeches brought the house down, this one shook the mountains. When the pope finished, young people stood and jumped and cheered and waved banners more than ever before.

But if that was the public John Paul II—the pope and the preacher—at his best, the next thing that happened showed the personal John Paul II—the priest and minister. Before the Mass had even started, I noticed one particular group of young people, up front but off to the same side of the stage that I was sitting on. They seemed particularly happy, particularly animated—not acting up or anything, but just glad to be there. One member of this group stood out. He appeared to have some kind of physical disability; there was something jerky about the way he moved, as if he suffered from muscular dystrophy or some other disease. Despite his disability, he still seemed to be the leader of the group. He had a guitar, and before the pope's arrival, he had led the group in singing songs. When they were talking or joking around, the others seemed to look up to him, to like him.

Now, with the Mass under way, I looked over to the group and watched the young man. He seemed raptly attentive to all that was going on, following each prayer, making each response, singing along with the choir—again, not in an inappropriate way, not trying to attract any attention. He just seemed . . . well, very involved in the service. At various parts of the service, when the choir was singing or someone else was performing one of the readings, the pope would come over and sit in an armchair only a few feet away from where I was sitting. He noticed this group—and this young man—as well. I could see him looking in their direction, squinting into the sun, watching them. I didn't know what to make of it.

The pope returned to the altar to continue the Mass. When it came time for Communion, he took the ciborium from the altar and turned to face the line who had been chosen to receive the Eucharist from him. At ever papal Mass, a certain number of people—fifty to one hundred—are privileged to receive the Eucharist from the Holy Father. They are seated in the front center section and are given special tickets. Great care is taken to make sure no one else is allowed to approach the altar. But as I watched those lucky enough to have been selected approach the Holy Father, I noticed that the boy from the group I had been watching was in the line now, clutching one of the precious tickets in his hand. I'm not sure of this, but my hunch is that the pope noticed the young man, saw his obvious and genuine devotion, and sent someone out into the audience with a ticket for him. I watched as the young man knelt in front of the Holy Father to receive Communion, his eyes closed and tears running down his cheeks.

As soon as the Mass was over, I hurried to Stapleton Airport to meet Vice President Al Gore, who had flown in to see the pope off. We waited for quite a while in a reception room that the airport made available to us. Gore's ten-year-old son, Albert Jr., was with us, the boy who had been hit by a car coming out of a baseball game at Camden Yards in Baltimore and injured so badly that his father passed up running for president in 1992. Thankfully, the boy had completely recovered. When we got word that the pope's motorcade was entering the airport, young Albert was taken into another room. A few minutes later, the pope arrived. I introduced him to the vice president and remarked to the Holy Father how well the trip had gone and how positively the young people had responded to his message. "Young people want to be good . . . in America and everywhere," he said. "And they like to be reminded that they should be good. They need to be reminded, like the flowers in the mountains need the rain and the sun."

I left the Holy Father and the vice president alone for their brief private meeting. After about fifteen minutes, I was called back in, and as I entered the room, I heard Vice President Gore ask the Holy Father if he had time to meet some of his staff—and his son. The Holy Father looked tired, which was no surprise considering the grueling schedule he had kept during his trip, but he didn't hesitate for a second. "Of course," he said. "Of course. I would be happy to." The three of us then went into the room next door. About ten or twenty members of the vice president's staff were there, and everyone stood up—everybody but the vice president's son. He was off in a corner, reading the comics in a newspaper that was spread out on a table in front of him. He was so lost in what he was doing that he hadn't even looked up when we came in.

"Albert," the vice president said. But the boy still didn't look up. The vice president said his son's name again, more sharply this time: "Albert!" Still no reaction. Then the pope swung into action. With a playful smile on his face, he went over and stood behind the boy, reading over his shoulder. It was a great scene—the vice president's photographer tiptoed over and took a picture of it—and it lasted for at least a couple of minutes. Finally, Al Gore Jr. must have "felt" someone behind him. When he looked up and saw who it was, his face filled with a wide-eyed look of surprise and wonder! It was fitting end of a trip for World Youth Day.

On the plane ride back to Rome from Denver, I was invited up front into the pope's cabin. The Holy Father was wearing his white cassock and slippers, and no skullcap. He motioned for me to sit down next to him. "I am very pleased with this trip," he told me. "The meeting with your president went well. I had the chance to meet your vice president. But the young people . . . the young people . . ." His voice trailed off. "It was so encouraging to see and to meet the young people of America. I feel I know them better now, better than the television or the newspapers. I leave with much hope for your beautiful country, for its future, after meeting so many beautiful young people in the United States."

I went back to my seat in the midsection of the plane, pleased and proud to have been a witness to this latest, triumphant visit to America by a still strong, still vibrant, still incredibly popular John Paul II.

10

FOLLOWING IN HIS FOOTSTEPS

To understand him, you have to understand where he came from

In October 1993, I was invited to speak at an International Human Rights Conference in Kraków, Poland. I took advantage of my trip to find out more about John Paul II by visiting the places where he had grown up and by talking to people who had known him as a boy, a young man, and a priest.

The night before I left Rome for Poland, I saw the Holy Father at a concert in Paul VI Hall that was held to mark the fourteenth anniversary of his pontificate. He was in good spirits, smiling, waving, and blessing the crowd before the concert, and afterward coming down from the stage and greeting as many people as he could. Kathy and I got a chance to speak to him in an impromptu receiving line. I wished him a happy anniversary and told him I was leaving for Poland the next day and that I would be visiting Kraków and Wadowice "and meeting some of your old friends."

The pope's eyes lit up. First he smiled, then he seemed to sigh, as if he wished it was that easy for him, to just jump on a plane and go home for a visit. "Wonderful!" he said. "I wish I could go with you!" He didn't say anything for a second, as if lost in thought, then he told me, "Take a warm coat. Winter comes sooner to Poland."

The pope asked me who I was going to see on my trip. I told him that the U.S. consulate was arranging a luncheon for me in Kraków and that, although I didn't know the names of everyone invited, I knew that Jerzy Turowicz, the editor of *Tygodnik Powszechny*, the Catholic newspaper that first published the young Father Wojtyla's writings, would be there. So would Tad Szulc, who was working on a biography of the pope. "That's wonderful," the pope repeated. "Remember me to them, especially Turowicz. Give them all my very warm regards."

"If I know the Polish people," I said, "we will sing *Stolat* to you," referring to the Polish song that goes "may you live to be a hundred . . ."

"Oh, yes." The pope laughed. "*Stolat*. Tell them I said *Stolat* to all of them." He moved on then, to others in the crowd, but he seemed preoccupied, as if he were still thinking of Poland.

After arriving in Kraków, I drove to Wadowice, a small town thirty miles to the southwest where Karol Wojtyla was born on May 18, 1920. There were about ten thousand people in Wadowice when he was growing up there, and there are not many more today. When I arrived, I met a priest whom people at the Vatican had suggested I contact. He had agreed to serve as my host and translator. He spoke English very well and seemed to know everyone in town.

Our first stop was 7 Koscienina Street where Karol Wojtyla was born; a small, stucco-covered building in the old town. The three-room apartment on the second floor is now a museum, preserved much as it was when the Wojtyla family lived there. You enter from an outside curving iron staircase, and the first thing you see is a holy water font by the door. Inside, the rooms are furnished simply with dark, solid-looking, wood furniture and holy pictures adorning the walls. A small altar is set up in the corner of the living room. There was a guide there, and she told us about the house. She said that when young Karol lived there it had been owned by a Jewish family, the Balamuths, who ran a store on the first floor and lived in an apartment in back. (I found out later that Yechiel Balamuth, his wife, and three of their daughters died in Nazi concentration camps.)

Upstairs, the guide said, and across the hall from the Wojtylas, lived another Jewish family, the Beers. Ginka Beer was two years older than Karol, a beautiful girl and a good student. She was usually the leading lady in high school and amateur theater productions, and Karol was often her leading man. A quarter of Wadowice's population was Jewish back then, the guide explained. (Subsequently, I learned that most people said the reason there was little anti-Semitism in the town was because the priests, especially Father Leonard Prochownik, wouldn't tolerate it. I also discovered that Ginka Beer, who moved with her family to Israel just in time to escape the Holocaust, said there was one family in Wadowice that showed no prejudice at all: her neighbors, the Wojtylas.)

The pope's father, Karol Sr., had been a tailor before making a career in the Polish army. Townspeople called him "the lieutenant," and he is described by everyone who knew him as a stern but fair man, a devout Catholic, and a student of Polish history. The pope's mother, Emilia Kaczorowska, was also a devout Catholic, but her health was not strong. Karol was the youngest child. A brother, Edmund, was fourteen years older. A sister, born six years before Karol, died a few weeks after birth. Karol's mother died when he was eight years old. His father, by then retired from the army, raised his son alone, cooking and taking care of the house. He mended Karol's clothes and even made suits and coats for him out of old army uniforms. The two of them ate breakfast and the evening meal in the small kitchen of their apartment, the guide told us, and most of their main, midday meals in a restaurant down the street.

The priest and I then visited the restaurant. When Karol was a boy, we were told, it had been run by the Banas family. One of the Banas sons went to school with Karol—and almost shot him accidentally when they were teenagers and playing with a gun. Today, the restaurant is decorated with tributes to the town's "favorite son, John Paul II." Pictures of him as a boy, a young man, a priest, a bishop, and a pope are hung on all the walls, and all sorts of memorabilia—books, a soccer ball, clothes—are displayed on shelves and in glass cases. It was the kind of shrine to a local hero you might expect to see in neighborhood or a small town in America, except here it would be a tribute to a famous athlete or movie star. There it was for a patriot and a pope.

The restaurant served very good Polish food—*pierogi, golumbki, kielbasa*—the kind I remembered from growing up in the Polish section of South Boston. We sat at a table and ordered a meal, then the priest began introducing me to some of the townspeople, people who had known "Lolek," as they called him, growing up. They were all very eager to talk about him, especially a group of elderly people who had gathered at the restaurant to plan an upcoming church festival.

"Karol was just like all of us growing up," one of them said, "playing, swimming in the river, playing sports. He was a good athlete, a good goalie in soccer."

But another man sitting across from him at the table disagreed: "He wasn't that good. I scored goals against him."

"He let you," the first man answered, smiling. "He was generous even then." And both of them laughed.

"A good student," someone else told us. "Always number one in the class."

"But he wouldn't let us copy his schoolwork," another said. "He would help us with our own, but he wouldn't let us copy his."

I asked if he was popular as a boy, if he ever got into trouble. One of them answered: "The only thing some of us didn't like was when our mothers would say, 'Why can't you be more like Lolek?'"

"But we didn't resent him for it," another said. "We all got along. We were always joking and singing songs."

"He became more serious," one of them said, "after his brother died." The pope's brother, who had become a doctor, died when Karol was twelve years old, after contracting scarlet fever from a patient he was treating.

"Karol went to church more after that," someone said.

"Did you know he was going to be someone important?" I asked.

"We all knew he was special, even back then," one answered. "He was so smart. But we thought he would become a professor—or an actor, because was in all the plays. We knew he would do *something*—but we just never thought he would be pope. Who ever thought there would be a Polish pope?"

I learned even more the next day at a luncheon in Kraków that the U.S. consul arranged for me. The luncheon took place at the home of one of the embassy staff, a town house in the old section of the city. The place was nicely furnished and had obviously been completely renovated. The walls were painted white; the dark woodwork had been restored. I was a little late arriving, and was shown into a dining room. There were about ten people already there, all men except for one woman, all of them old friends of the pope. They were sitting around a long oval table, on top of which were piled platters of steaming Polish food. They had just begun to eat.

Tad Szulc, a Polish-born, former *New York Times* reporter who was working on a biography of John Paul II at the time, was there, which was lucky for me because a lot of the conversation was in Polish and Tad was able to translate for me. I was introduced to everyone, although I didn't get all of their names. Jerzy Turowicz's name was the only one familiar to me. In addition to publishing the first articles by then Father Wojtyla, beginning in 1949, Turowicz had become one of the leading intellectuals in Poland, working closely with Solidarity and the new, freely elected government. The rest of those at the table were academics and professionals. A number were university professors, one was a doctor, one ran some kind of a small press or publishing house. Like the people in the restaurant in Wadowice, they were very glad to talk about their old friend, which they did in both Polish and English. I noticed, though, that it seemed their funniest stories were always in Polish. I assumed they were remembrances they didn't think it was appropriate to share with an "outsider."

The old friends talked about Karol Wojtyla in his student days and his ability as a student and as an actor.

"What a memory!" one said. "Not only would he memorize his own lines, the lines of the leading actor, but he would know our lines, too. And he would remind us if we forgot."

I asked them what he was like in college. "Oh, the poet!" one said. "He looked like a poet and dressed like one, too. Long hair. Clothes in the bohemian style."

I was curious about what it had been like when the Germans invaded. Now the talk became more serious.

"They came on that Sunday," one explained. "They closed the university, took many of the teachers away. We never saw them again. Monday, when we came for class, they told us to go home, that we must all go to work, that there was no more time for school, that we had to help them win the war."

Everyone had to go to work then, they told me. Karol labored in a quarry first, then in a chemical plant. But he and some of the others would meet secretly in people's houses—with professors to study, or in an underground theater company, putting on plays in people's living rooms.

"After a while," one explained, "Karol didn't come around as much. His father died, and he began studying to be a priest. Some of his friends from the theater tried to talk him out of it but his mind was made up. We didn't see him so much after that."

One of the men, a professor, I think, came up with a particularly striking image then: "It was as if he was trying on different lives—the poet, the actor, the worker, the priest. And then after that, well, he just kept going—the bishop, the cardinal, the pope."

It occurred to me that one of the reasons for the special nature of this pope could be that he was a man of the world before he was a man of the cloth. Not only did he audition for different roles, he also had women friends and must have thought about marriage and a family, about having a wife and children—before he sacrificed these things to devote his life to Christ. I didn't know if there was an exact moment that Karol Wojtyla decided to become a priest. Certainly no one at this table could come up with one. But I think it's important to understand the competing emotions that he must have felt. It seemed to me his decision was the product of the kind of healthy debate that the best priests have with themselves. I knew that the Vatican wasn't comfortable with people speculating about the Holy Father's early life, that they would rather he be described as some kind of pious mystic—which he is. But he's also a real man, and that's what attracts me and so many people to him.

Most of their talk, though, had to do with the years under communism and how their friend, first as Father Wojtyla, then as a bishop and then a cardinal, handled himself. "I remember when he dropped off that first article," Turowicz said. "It was in the spring of 1949. I didn't expect much from this young priest, but then I read it—all about priests organizing the dockworkers in France and how that was the logical extension of Catholic social teaching. I ran it on the front page." When he said "dockworkers," my ears perked up. That was what had sparked my interest in John Paul II almost fifteen years before, when I first met him —his interest in dockworkers like my father and my wife's father. Now, here I was, talking to someone who knew him back then.

"He fooled them into letting him become a bishop," someone else at the table said, referring to Poland's communist regime. "They didn't know who they were getting." They all talked of him outfoxing the communist government and somehow being able to build new churches, open new seminaries, and celebrate Mass—and what this meant to the people of Poland.

"The only freedom allowed was in the church—so that's where people went to have their freedom," Jerzy Turowicz explained. "You know that," he said to me. "We remember when you came, when you met Walesa and Mazowiecki at St. Brigid's. It was a dangerous time, so we appreciated your visit—and the fact that you brought your son."

I was taken aback. Turowicz was referring to the trip that I had made to Poland in 1988. It was obvious that these people had done their homework, that they had a scouting report on me.

Much of the talk concerned their friend's first trip back to Poland after becoming pope.

"Nobody thought they would let him come back. It was a big mistake—but we were glad they made it," one said, and the others around the table smiled and nodded in agreement. "And when everyone came out to see him—and nothing bad happened to them. When they saw how many there were of us and how few of them . . . well, that was the beginning of the end. Once the door was opened, you couldn't close it anymore."

Jerzy Turowicz had the last word on the subject: "Historians say World War II ended in 1945. Maybe in the rest of the world, but not in Poland. They say communism fell in 1989. Not in Poland. World War II and communism both ended in Poland at the same time—in 1979, when John Paul II came home."

I asked them how much they saw of him now that he was pope, and they all brightened up.

"When he came back in 1979, he was like a king," one said. "And to be able to see him then—and in his other visits—that was a grand thing."

"But the reunion was best," another offered. In November 1988, I learned, the pope hosted a fiftieth high school reunion in Rome.

"We thought we might see him once or twice," one of his old classmates told me, "but we ate every meal with him. He wouldn't let us call him Holy Father or Your Holiness or anything—just Lolek or Karol. And he wouldn't let us kiss his ring. We just talked about our school days and sang songs." They were describing the scene the way you would expect anyone to talk about a high school friend who had made good but hadn't forgotten his old friends.

While I was in Kraków, I visited the Rakowicki Cemetery, where the pope's mother, father, and brother are buried. It was a very cold afternoon, and I was met at the gates of the cemetery by the mayor of Kraków Province, and a number of other Polish government officials, as well as the U.S. consul. They showed me to the Wojtyla plot, and we laid two wreaths of carnations at the foot of the headstone: one was of red, white, and blue flowers in the design of the American flag; the other contained red and white flowers in the design of the Polish flag. A priest was there, and he conducted a very simple and respectful service, which, because of the pope's devotion to the Blessed Mother, including singing the *Regina Coeli*—Hail Holy Queen. When the ceremony was over, I was given a tour of the cemetery. I was struck by the thousands and thousands of small headstones, row after row after row, marked with the dates 1942, 1943, and 1944. I was also struck by large headstones in open areas, with no names on them, only a single date. I was told that they were mass graves. Priests weren't allowed to conduct services during the day under the Nazis, so they had to sneak into the cemetery to conduct Christian burials in the middle of the night, knowing that if they were caught they would be jailed—or shot. This, I realized, was what it was like in Poland when Karol Wojtyla decided to become a priest.

I got a chance to learn more about Father Wojtyla from the priest who had shown me around Wadowice. After our tour, he drove me out to the church being built for his parish, just outside the town. We walked through the church, where the construction was nearly complete, and then went back into the sacristy, behind the altar, where more work still had to be done. There, he introduced me to an older priest who had known Karol Wojtyla growing up. This priest was a real character, with a mischievous sense of humor.

"Karol was lucky," the old priest said with a grin. "The only difference between us was that he could hear better than me. He heard God call him after the Nazis came. It took me ten years more. I didn't hear God call me until after the Communists came. I guess God's voice doesn't travel so well down in the mines." During the war, and for years after that, he explained, he had been a coal miner in Nowa Huta. "But I am lucky, too, because now I know a pope."

He and the young priest told me more. "At one point, Karol wanted to leave the seminary to become a Carmelite monk," the older one said, "so that he could fast and pray all day. But the cardinal wouldn't let him. He said the church in Poland needed priests more than it needed monks. And he was correct. Think of the loss to the church if this man had spent all his life behind the walls of a monastery."

"In his first parish," the young priest added, "they say Father Wojtyla slept on a board and dressed in old clothes and secondhand cassocks. And when people gave him anything better, he gave it away to the poor." The young priest said the future pope had possessed a "gift" for working with young people, with college students: "He would take them on camping trips in the mountains, and use nature to bring them closer to God and their faith."

The human rights conference in Kraków, was held at the pope's alma mater, Jagiellonian University. There I learned more about the pope's early career from a longtime Catholic scholar who had known Karol Wojtyla from the time he became a bishop in 1958. The only reason

the Communist government allowed Father Wojtyla to become aux-
iliary bishop of Kraków, this man told me, after turning down six
other candidates, was because officials thought he was an intellectual
and not someone who was interested in politics or who would cause
them any trouble. But they were in for a surprise! "He asked them for
permission to build new churches," the professor told me, "and when
they wouldn't give it to him, he held Masses on the vacant lots where
he wanted those churches to be. Thousands of people came to those
outdoor Masses, because it was a way for them to protest against the
government. Finally the Communists let him build the churches.
They figured it would be less of a threat if they could get the people
inside where nobody could see them."

I met another old friend of the Holy Father's—and of mine—at
the conference: Lech Walesa. In August 1988, when I was mayor of
Boston, I visited Poland when Walesa was leading Solidarity workers
in the famous strike at the Lenin Shipyard in Gdansk. When I asked
for permission to meet Walesa it was denied, but it took more than
that to stop me from meeting one of the great worker heroes of this
century. Using the street smarts of my native South Boston, I managed to get myself and my son Eddie smuggled into the shipyard by
hiding under a pile of blankets on the back of an open flatbed truck.
This was the first time I had seen Walesa since that adventure, five
years before.

"You have come back!" Walesa said, greeting me with a hug and a
big smile under his bushy mustache.

"I'm working with your friend the pope now," I said.

"He's everybody's friend," Walesa replied, still shaking my hand.

"The thing I still remember," I told Walesa, "was that when I first
met you, you were wearing his picture pinned to your shirt."

"He gave us the strength." Walesa nodded and his face turned
serious. "He helped us believe that what we were doing was possible. If a Pole can become pope . . . than anything is possible. If
the Polish pope can come home to Poland . . . then the Polish people
can be free. That was his message to us, especially that first time, in
1979."

Walesa delivered his speech and I delivered mine. Afterwards, I found out that the auditorium where we spoke—Juliusz Slowacki Theater—was named for one of Karol Wojtyla's favorite poets and playwrights, and that, as a high school student, Karol Wojtyla had attended many plays there, including one that was about the election of a Slavic pope.

11

RUNNING FOR POPE

Trust the Holy Spirit—but line up the votes

Whenever we could, Kathy and I would explore other parts of Italy, taking weekend trips north and south of Rome. One weekend, we made a trip to *San Giovanni Rotondo*, near Naples, to visit the monastery where Padre Pio, a Capuchin monk and mystic, had lived and preached. The lines of people there to attend Mass and receive the sacraments were enormous. Luckily, though, we got a private tour, which included having lunch with an old priest, Father Allesio, who had taken care of Padre Pio before the old monk died in 1968. He told us the following story.

In 1947, while he was on Easter vacation from the Angelicum College in Rome, Father Karol Wojtyla and another priest traveled to *San Giovanni Rotondo*. After Mass, the two priests lined up along with thousands of other pilgrims at *Casa Sollievo della Sofferenza* (the House of Relief and Suffering) for confession with Padre Pio. After hearing Wojtyla's confession, however, the little monk with the long white beard fell to his knees and prophesied that this young Polish priest would one day become pope. He also foretold that someone would try to assassinate him.

It's a remarkable story, a story that, I've been told, the pope doesn't confirm but won't deny. To me, though, maybe because I'm a politician, the fact *that* Karol Wojtyla became pope isn't as interesting as *how* he came to be pope.

But speculating on how this pope—or any pope—went about being elected was one thing. Getting anyone at the Vatican to talk about the subject was quite another. One day, though, I was able to get what American newspapers call a "reliable source" to open up a little on the subject.

Giuseppe Cardinal Caprio had been *sostituto,* a kind of chief of staff, to Paul VI. He was now retired but living in Rome and still very familiar with the ways of the Vatican. One afternoon, he did me the favor of sharing a little of his wisdom with me.

We had lunch outdoors, in the garden of Villa Richardson. Although it was late October, it was a warm day, leaves were still on the trees, and late flowers were in bloom. We had finished eating, and over cappuccino, I asked Cardinal Caprio to explain to me how Karol Wojtyla, or anyone, went about becoming pope.

"Well, first of all, the Holy Spirit guides the College of Cardinals in choosing someone," the cardinal said, delivering the usual Vatican party line. "But second, the *papabili*, the candidates, work at it." He said, beginning to open up, "There must be the inspiration from above. But down below, there must be talent, hard work, and also opportunity. For this pope, the opportunity was Vatican II. Before that, he might have been well known in his circle of academics and intellectuals in Poland. But at Vatican II, he got a chance to show himself—not just to Rome but to the whole church, the whole world."

Cardinal Caprio told me that most church officials thought Vatican II was going to be just a "one-time occurrence to reaffirm church doctrine and take care of some loose ends," but that it turned into more than that—it became a four-year struggle to redefine the church in the modern world. "Wojtyla was right in the middle of it," he said, "the changes in the liturgy, the value of the human person, the idea that the church should be more of an advocate for religious freedom and human rights, not only for Catholics but for everyone. And the junior cardinal from Poland really made a name for himself."

"But how? How does it work?" I asked him.

"Well," he said, "it's like anything, any organization, any business or political party. You watch, you listen, you meet people, you show them what you are capable of doing. He did all that. Before the council, he wrote lots of memoranda. At the council, he worked on committees. Afterward, he went around meeting people—at dinners and where they were staying. In between sessions, he did the grunt work, drafting the reports and getting them to his colleagues for comments. He showed everyone his talents, his skills. Some people call that a sign of ambition. Some call it a sign of working hard for God and His church."

"And that's what Wojtyla did?" I asked.

"He wasn't the only one," the cardinal replied, "but he was one of the shining lights. He got himself, his name, and his ideas out there. He attended each session. He spoke or submitted papers at every opportunity. His name was in the papers. He was heard on radio. He did radio broadcasts back to Poland to explain what was going on at the council. People got to know him and they were impressed with him. He was a rising star. Then, after the first session, John XXIII died and his successor, Paul VI, took a special interest in this young Polish bishop."

"Why him?" I asked. "Why not somebody else?"

"For a couple of reasons," the cardinal replied. "Paul wanted to continue John's foreign policy, the *Ostpolitik*, of talking with Communist governments instead of refusing to deal with them, as Pius XII had done. Wojtyla was in the middle of all that in Poland, negotiating with Communists there over building churches and seminaries. And he was easier to deal with than the primate, Cardinal Wyszynski. The other thing was that the commission the pope had appointed to look into birth control came back with a report that said they couldn't find anything in the Bible against it! That put the pope in a box, and he turned to Wojtyla—who had written a book about marriage and sexuality—to help him get out of it."

Cardinal Caprio told me how Wojtyla had helped draft Paul VI's landmark encyclical *Humanae Vitae*, which denounced not only abortion but birth control as well. The pope was grateful for then-bishop Wojtyla's help and showed it—by making him one of the youngest cardinals in the church. After that, they continued to have a close relationship.

"But just because you have a good relationship with a pope doesn't make you a pope yourself," I suggested.

"No, but it doesn't hurt," the cardinal answered. "The other thing that puts your name in the hat is getting to know your fellow cardinals. You do that by working hard at the councils and synods like Wojtyla did—and by traveling, which he also did."

"Traveling?" I pursued.

"Yes, traveling. It gets you around. It helps you to meet people, powerful people who someday might be helpful to you. It's the closest thing the church has to what you could call campaigning, whether for pope or any other job. Wojtyla went to the Holy Land with some other bishops the year before the pope did, in 1964. He went to Canada and the United States twice. He went to the Philippines and Australia. He got to know cardinals and bishops from all over the world and the problems they faced in their countries—and he invited them to come to Poland to see what he was up against and the things he was doing under difficult circumstances."

I thought back to my first meeting with Cardinal Wojtyla in 1969. Even though I was running for office myself at the time, I hadn't thought that his visit had any "political" implications within the church. Now, I realized, that it had.

"It makes sense," Cardinal Caprio continued. "Somebody with an intellect like his, a life story like his, a commitment like his . . . Well, there's no sense in keeping that kind of light under a bushel basket."

"So, what you're saying, Your Eminence, is that people actually *run* for pope?" I asked.

"They don't run *for* it—but they don't run *away from* it, either," the elderly cardinal answered with a smile. "Even the one before this one, John Paul I, did. They say he didn't want the job, but a copy of his book was placed by the door of every cardinal in the conclave. The Holy Spirit didn't put them there."

Cardinal Caprio finished his cappuccino. He also finished talking. I hoped he didn't think he had said too much or talked too freely. I didn't think there was anything disrespectful in anything he had said. I was very grateful for all he had shared with me. It greatly helped me to understand the church, the papacy, and the man better—and gave me even more reason to respect the current pope.

The cardinal thanked me for lunch and we got up from the table and walked through the garden and into the house. Here I was, the so-called politician, but I felt as though I'd just gotten a lesson in Politics 101, Vatican-style.

Since the cardinal didn't have a driver or a car, I had my embassy driver give him a ride home. I went along to share a few more minutes with him. Driving through Rome, with the *polizia* in front of us waving cars out of our way, the cardinal pointed out different places—the Angelicum, where Father Wojtyla attended graduate school; the Belgian College, where he lived. As he stepped out of the car, the cardinal bent down and imparted a few last words of wisdom: "You've heard the expression, *Ambasciatore*, 'Heaven helps those who help themselves.' Well, in a conclave, the Holy Spirit helps those who help themselves."

12

PIAZZA DI SPAGNA

A special day—and a special devotion to Mary

I took advantage of every opportunity I could to see the pope in action and to hear what he was talking about. Every Wednesday, I would go to his general audience, held either outside, in St. Peter's Square, or inside Paul VI Hall. Every Sunday, Kathy and I would walk down the Janiculum Hill to St. Peter's to hear his Angelus message. If he spoke only in Italian, I'd drop by the Vatican Press Office on the *Via della Conciliazione*, leading to the square to pick up a translation of his words. If he was celebrating special Masses or feast days, I would try to be present. If you worked at it—and I did—you could see him in action and hear him speak three or four times a week. I also read *L'Osservatore Romano* faithfully, both the English-language version and translations of articles from the larger, Italian editions. *Vaticanisti* (Vatican watchers) had told me you had to do all this to keep on top of things. They compared watching the pope and reading the paper carefully—both for what was said and what wasn't—to Kremlin-watching or reading the wall posters in China under Mao.

I want to be clear about this, though: I didn't follow the pope this closely just because I had contracted a serious case of hero worship—although I admit it was always a thrill to be in his presence. I did it because it helped me do my job. The pope didn't waste any events. He used every one to speak out on issues and themes that were on his mind, and I saw being there and keeping my eyes and ears open as the best way to keep up with the latest thinking of the Holy See. It also helped me to get to know the Holy Father better as a human being.

Take December 8, 1993, the Feast of the Immaculate Conception. It was a beautiful, sunny day, and an especially busy day for me. I began by attending the annual luncheon at the North American College, the seminary, for students from the United States and Canada, that is sometimes called the American Catholic Church's West Point. My wife, Kathy, delivered the traditional toast to the President of the United States, the first woman to do so since Clare Boothe Luce. But first she had a little fun with the rector, our good friend Monsignor Tim Dolan. Tim's quite a conservative, even in church circles, and after he graciously introduced Kathy, she praised him as an "ardent liberal feminist." This caused Tim to blush cardinal red and the seminarians to whoop it up with laughter.

Coincidentally, during lunch I was called from the table to take a phone call from President Clinton himself. He asked if I could host a dinner party that night for Haitian Prime Minister Robert Malval and his wife—something I was able to pull off thanks to the efforts of my daughters, who did all the cooking and serving, since it was a holiday for the household staff.

After the luncheon, Kathy and I attended our next event—the annual Solemnity of the Immaculate Conception and the crowning of the statue of the Blessed Virgin Mary at the *Piazza di Spagna*. I had heard it was one of the Holy Father's favorite events, and so I especially wanted to be there.

December 8th is both a holy day and a national holiday in Italy. Schools, banks, and shops are closed, and thousands turn out for the ceremony at the *Piazza di Spagna*. The piazza is formed by the intersection of a number of narrow streets and surrounded on all sides by seventeenth- and eighteenth-century earth- and pastel-colored buildings. This square is busier than most. At one end are the famous Spanish Steps, a popular tourist attraction and meeting place for young people. At the other end is the Congregation of the Propagation of Faith. In recent years, one of the busiest McDonald's restaurants in Europe opened up directly across the street, a situation that the prefect, Josef Cardinal Tomko of Slovakia, told me he was not at all pleased with. In the center of the piazza is a fifty-foot high obelisk, on top of which is a statue of a haloed Virgin Mary. Every year on December 8th, the statue is crowned with a wreath of flowers in a very unique way: a Roman firefighter is hoisted up at the end of the ladder by an aerial fire truck. The ceremony is very popular with Romans and tourists, and thousands turn out to pack the streets leading into the square.

Kathy and I had arrived early to attend a reception at the residence of the Spanish ambassador to the Holy See, which is located right across the street from the monument to Our Lady. December 8th is also a national holiday in Spain, and every year the Spanish ambassador hosts a National Day party for the rest of the diplomatic community. The ambassador's residence is a huge, umber-colored villa taking up most of one side of the square. The reception was held in what the Italians call the first-floor (we would call it the second floor) ballroom, where tall, floor-to-ceiling windows with balconies overlooked the square and the statue.

The plan was for everyone at the reception to gather at the windows when the pope arrived and to watch the veneration ceremony from that vantage point. But I didn't want to be even that far away. I liked to take advantage of every opportunity to see this pope at work, the closer the better. So, Kathy and I went downstairs and—thanks to some effective blocking by my embassy security staff—we made our way outside, across the street, and into the barricaded area around the monument. There, we met the Spanish ambassador and his wife, and the recently elected mayor of Rome, Francesco Rutelli, as well as the Roman firefighters taking part in the ceremony.

After waiting for twenty minutes or so, we began to hear cries of *"Viva il Papa! Viva il Papa!"* echoing off the stucco walls of the ancient buildings, then the sound of applause, gradually getting closer and closer. In a few minutes, the pope's motorcade came into view, inching its way through the crowd. Four police motorcyclists were in the lead, gunning their engines and herding the crowd out of the way like border collies herding sheep. Then two police cruisers followed, blue lights flashing from the roofs and sirens buzzing. Next came the pope's black Mercedes, flanked by dark-suited security officers on foot. Two cars of *polizia* brought up the rear. Now the shouts of the crowd were loudest: *"Viva il Papa! Viva il Papa!"*

Finally, the pope's Mercedes pulled up alongside us. When the doors opened, I saw the Holy Father, along with Monsignor Dziwisz and Cardinal Camillo Ruini, the Vicar General of Rome. Those two stepped out of the car first, then the pope got out, assisted by Monsignor Dziwisz. The reason the Holy Father needed help was that he'd tripped on a new piece of carpeting a few weeks before after addressing a U.N. group and had dislocated his right shoulder. Now, as the Holy Father walked toward us, I saw that his shoulder was in a sling and that his face was a grimace of pain. He tried to hide it, forcing a smile, but you could see by the way he moved, tipped over a little to one side, that he was favoring his injured shoulder. He waved a blessing to the crowd with his left hand, and then, surrounded by a convoy of priests who had appeared at his side, settled down to business.

The pope led the opening series of prayers, lowering himself down to a kneeler placed near the base of the statue. After the prayers and some songs by a choir standing nearby, the wreath was brought over, and the pope blessed it, again using his left hand to make the sign of the cross. The wreath was then handed to one of the Roman firefighters, who stepped over to the aerial truck and mounted the ladder.

Inside the cab of the truck, the operator set some levers in motion, and the ladder started to uncoil, sending the firefighter slowly some fifty feet into the air. When he got to the right height, the end of the ladder was maneuvered so the firefighter was face-to-face with the statue of the Blessed Virgin. He raised the wreath, placed it on top of the halo of the statue, and fastened it on. When he pulled his hands away, a cheer arose from the crowd.

"Viva Maria! Viva Madonna!" the crowd cheered, before turning its attention back to the Holy Father. *"Viva il Papa! Viva il Papa!"* The pope turned to the crowd and raised his good arm and shook his hand up and down, motioning for quiet. When the firefighter returned to earth and the engine of the fire truck was shut off, the pope led the crowd in more prayers and songs in tribute to the Blessed Mother. His voice seemed to become stronger the more he spoke.

When the ceremony ended, the Holy Father blessed the crowd. The chants of *"Viva il Papa!"* resumed. This time the pope did nothing to quiet them. Instead, he turned toward the Spanish ambassador's residence across the street and waved to the members of the diplomatic corps, standing and watching in the windows. They waved back and applauded him. The pope then turned his attention to those of us inside the barricades with him. First he greeted the Spanish ambassador and his wife, then the mayor of Rome, Francesco Rutelli, then he turned to Kathy and me. Even though his voice had grown stronger and more resonant as the ceremony proceeded, I saw that his shoulder still bothered him and he had to work to keep a sort of half-smile on his face. But he seemed determined to not let the injury slow him down or force him to retreat into the Vatican before he was ready.

"Ambassador," he said, stepping over to me and extending his left hand for me to shake. "I see you everywhere. You are following me, no?" he joked. Then, more seriously, "Today is a very special day for your country. Mary, the mother of Christ, is the patron saint of the United States as well. I have heard that many of America's soldiers, in time of danger, in time of battle, have turned to Our Mother Mary for help. I have heard it said that some even wrap a rosary around their rifles so they can pray when they are in battle."

I'd never heard of that, but I had heard of people whose lives were saved when bullets were stopped by "pocket rosaries" tucked in shirt pockets. I told the pope two such stories, one involving a soldier and one a police officer. Then I pulled out the pocket rosary that I always carry. (A pocket rosary is a small metal disk with five knobs protruding, each representing a decade of the rosary.) The pope looked at it in my hand for a few seconds, then he took it from me, in his left hand. He studied it, rubbing it between his thumb and forefinger. I couldn't tell whether or not the pope was familiar with this kind of a rosary. He seemed lost in thought. I had no way of knowing what he was thinking, of course, but I wondered if the rosary and the stories brought him back to that day in St. Peter's Square in 1981 when an assassin's bullet almost cost him his life. I knew he credited the intercession of the Blessed Mother for allowing him to survive the attack and that he'd brought the bullet to the shrine of Fatima in Portugal and left it in the crown of Mary's statue there. I didn't know then—

and wouldn't know until seven years later, when the whole world would find out—that the third prophecy of Fatima involved an attack on the "bishop in white." The Holy Father did know, though; even before the assassination attempt he was aware of the warning.

The pope's eyes were closed. His lips were moving. All I could think was that he was saying Hail Marys. After a long pause, the Holy Father opened his eyes and looked at me again. He gave the rosary back to me, and when I had it in my hand, he blessed it. "Let us remember everything Mary has done," he said, "for each of us and for all of us by becoming the mother of Christ."

He stepped away then, and was surrounded by Cardinal Ruini, Monsignor Dziwisz, and others who helped him into his car. It took a long time for the motorcade to get going again, and then to make its way back through the crowds that were once again chanting *"Viva il Papa! Viva il Papa!"* Finally, his car disappeared. But for a long time afterward the sound of the cheering continued.

13

DIPLOMATIC CORPS BRIEFING

Standing up for the U.S.A.

Once someone is nominated for an ambassadorship—and while they are going through the confirmation process—the U.S. State Department conducts a series of briefings for the candidate. The briefings are very useful for providing background information on international affairs. The briefings also cover diplomatic etiquette—where you stand, where you sit, how you address the people you are going to meet, that sort of thing. They try to cover all the bases. But as far as I was concerned, the briefings hadn't covered one very important subject for someone in my position—how to talk to the pope. That was something of particular concern for a Catholic like me, who didn't see this man as just a head of state but as Christ's representative on earth. Luckily, before leaving for Rome, I received a crash course on the subject from other—higher-placed—sources.

In June 1993, before I left Boston for Rome, Bernard Cardinal Law invited me to his residence on Lake Street in Brighton one evening to meet Monsignor Jim Harvey, head of what is called the "second section," the English-speaking section of the Vatican's foreign office. Monsignor Harvey was in Boston to receive treatment for a chronic eye problem at the Massachusetts Eye and Ear Clinic, and Cardinal Law thought it might be a good thing for us to get together. Kathy and I went over after going to a youth sporting event in Roxbury. We were shown into the cardinal's large dining room that looks out, through big windows, onto the campus of St. John's Seminary. It was a beautiful summer evening, and you could see the seminarians strolling the grounds. The nuns who help out at the cardinal's residence served coffee and homemade cookies—with walnuts, which they knew were my favorite. Then I had my first lesson in how to talk to a pope, or at least to this pope, John Paul II.

"Most people have trouble," Monsignor Harvey told us. "It's understandable. They're nervous. They're excited. They don't know what to say, so they end up blurting out some kind of pleasantry or triviality like 'I'm so happy to meet you, Holy Father.' Or 'That was a beautiful service, Holy Father.' Or 'What a great speech, Your Holiness.' Then, afterward, they're kicking themselves because they missed out on a chance to say something really meaningful or important. And the thing is," he continued, "the pope misses out, too. He loves to hear from people. He wants feedback, stimulation, information. He loves it when people say something to him that he can think about later. He'd rather have that any day."

Cardinal Law gave me another piece of advice. "Don't be afraid to talk shop," the cardinal told me. "Don't think you can't talk business when you see him. The Holy Father will expect you to use every opportunity to weigh in on things. It's not inappropriate to bring up something when you run into him. It's fair game. If there's something he needs to hear, he expects you to say it to him. He *wants* to hear it."

It was the best advice I received before taking the job, and I tried to follow it whenever possible. Whether I had forty-five minutes with the pope, as I would at our first meeting at Castel Gandolfo, or forty-five seconds after an audience, a Mass, or a rosary, I tried to use that time to communicate with him. And I told other people—not just other diplomats but ordinary people—to do the same: "Say something you want him to know. Don't worry. He won't mind. He'll like it. And you'll still get your rosary blessed."

In January 1994, I attended the pope's annual address to the diplomatic corps for the first time, and had one of my first chances to put that advice to use. The event was held in the *Sala Regia*, the antechamber to the Sistine and Pauline Chapels and one of the most beautiful of the reception halls in the Apostolic Palace. The walls of the long, narrow room are covered with fifteenth-century frescoes, and the vaulted ceiling is covered in gold leaf. It's a very formal affair; diplomats wear white tie and tails or their traditional native uniforms, and the pope sits up on a throne wearing the red *mozzetta* and colorful vestments. It can be a very intimidating event, especially when the pope singles out your country for criticism.

The pope's theme that year was the dangers of nationalism, but in talking about various trouble spots around the world, he deplored the violence that had resulted in a clash between U.S. Marines and a rebel gang in Somalia. After he finished speaking, all the ambassadors formed a receiving line in order to say a few words to the pope—and I used my brief time with him to respond to what he had just said. "Holy Father," I said, "about Somalia. Our government is sending food, medicine, and clothes—but it is all being stolen by the warlords. Our soldiers were not sent in to fight—they were sent to protect the shipments, to see that they reached the people who need them."

The pope looked at me closely, but not crossly. He didn't seem offended. He knew I was just doing my job. But he also understood that I was offering a challenge to him, saying, in effect, "If you can come up with a better way to get the deliveries through, let's hear it." But by saying what he said next, he was telling me that wasn't *his* job. "I understand the difficulty," he said. "But we must not resort to violence. We want to end suffering, not create more of it." Leaving me to figure out how to do that, he continued down the line of diplomats.

14

SANTA SABINA

Not so much a pope as a priest among friends

One of the most beautiful and solemn traditions in Rome is for the pope to begin Lent by celebrating Ash Wednesday Mass at the Church of Santa Sabina, the ancient headquarters church of the Dominican Order on the Aventine Hill, just up the street from the U.S. embassy to the Holy See.

Santa Sabina was first established in the fifth century. The present church was built in the sixteenth century, but the monastery next door is even older. It was built by St. Dominic and St. Thomas Aquinas once lived there. The Ash Wednesday Mass is celebrated more for the religious community than for the public at large. Only a handful of the other ambassadors attended. I was a regular because of the strong ties I had with the Dominican Order of Preachers, the result of my graduating from Providence College and receiving the school's highest honor, the Veritas Medal. Most of those attending, though, were priests and nuns of the Dominican Order, and some from other communities as well. Because of this, it was said to be one of the favorite services of the year for the Holy Father.

John Paul II understands and appreciates, probably more than any of his recent predecessors, the *public* nature of the papacy. That's why he's so active, why he travels so much, why he uses the media—television, radio, newspaper, books, even the Internet—to reach out to people. That's why he pays attention to the style as well as the substance of his message. Sometimes, though, that public role can wear on him. I've seen an annoyed look cross the pope's face when people take his picture during Mass. I've heard that when people try to sneak into line to receive Communion from him, he's said something like "It is the body of Christ that is important, not who puts it on your tongue." That's probably why he liked Ash Wednesday at Santa Sabina. It was always a very beautiful, dignified, respectful religious service, attended by those more interested in giving glory to God than worrying about celebrities on earth. I was told that even as a student at the nearby Angelicum, the young Karol Wojtyla would attend the Santa Sabina service. "He always seemed to feel at home here," one of the Dominicans told me.

Santa Sabina is a beautiful church. The interior is lined in white marble. Stained-glass windows are set high up in the walls. The ceiling is paneled and decorated with gold stars. The altar is white marble, set before a vaulted apse. In front is a rectangular seating area surrounded by a low, white marble wall that I've seen in other churches, but I don't know what they're called. They're almost like the penalty boxes they have at hockey games. In Santa Sabina, this "box" is full of wooden pews and kneelers and reserved for the priests of the Dominican Order. Members of other orders and other visitors are seated in a small section of rows of folding chairs behind this box. Behind them are rows of chairs reserved for Dominican nuns in their white habits and black veils.

The first year I attended the service, I was sitting in the front row of the visitors' section. When the pope entered the church, he came forward along the center aisle, then skirted the box where the priests were standing and went along it to the altar. He officiated at a solemn Mass and afterward distributed ashes to the foreheads of the priests of the order as they came before him at the front of the altar. After the service, the pope made his way down from the altar and back through the church, leisurely greeting those in attendance. There was none of the pushing, shoving, or overexcitement that can sometime mar a service at St. Peter's. He was neither a celebrity nor a stranger here; he was part of the community, and he seemed to enjoy that. He wasn't rushing; he wasn't looking ahead to the next dignitary he had to greet. He seemed at peace.

There was a reception after the service in a room of the monastery adjoining the church, and the Holy Father attended for a few minutes. He was smiling, he looked relaxed. He didn't seem to be "working" or "watching himself." He knew many of the people there personally and was giving as many hugs as handshakes. An impromptu receiving line formed so people could have a word with the Holy Father, but again, it was very casual, very relaxed. There were no ushers keeping people in line or hurrying them along. When I stepped before the Holy Father, he greeted me warmly. "Ambassador," he said, "it is good to see you, especially here at Santa Sabina. It reminds me that you and I, we have something very much in common."

"What's that, Holy Father?" I asked, taking my cue from his manner and making a joke, "that we're both good Catholics?"

The pope smiled at my joke, nodding his head. "Yes," he said, "I hope we are both that. But something else. We were both taught by Dominicans." Then, looking around at a group of older Dominican priests—by older, I mean around the pope's age—he sighed playfully and added, "But I suspect we went to school at different times."

It was a very pleasant evening. The Holy Father stayed for a while, talking with the priests and nuns. As he was about to leave, he gave us all his blessing. Afterward, I stepped outside the church and watched him walk through the arched courtyard accompanied by Monsignor Dziwisz and some Dominicans. He stood by his car for a few minutes talking before getting in. It was an unusual setting in which to see the Holy Father; it was not so much of an event as an evening out with friends.

15

"WHERE IS RAYMOND'S FRIEND?"

Answering a dying boy's prayers

As effective as John Paul II was in front of large groups of people, he was even better with people individually, one on one. So, one of the most rewarding aspects of my job as Ambassador to the Holy See was being able to arrange for people to meet the pope.

Early on, I arranged for one of the Marines who was assigned to the security detail at the American Embassy—Corporal Joseph Pora, a Polish-American from Attleboro, Massachusetts—to attend the early morning Mass that the pope celebrates in his private chapel, the same service that Kathy and I had attended with Monsignor Stanislaw Sypek back in 1985. For weeks beforehand, Joe couldn't talk about anything else. When the day came, right after the Mass he rushed back to the embassy to call his mother, even though it was three A.M. back home. I overheard him talking a mile a minute over the phone—in Polish—to her. After he'd hung up, I asked him what his mother said. "Nothing," he told me. "She couldn't talk. She was crying too much."

Sometimes, arranging for someone to meet the pope is just plain fun. When the New York Yankees held a Phil Rizzuto Day at Yankee Stadium for their former shortstop and broadcaster, they showered him with the usual presents, like a new car and other material gifts. But when Rizzuto spoke, after thanking everyone and saying how lucky he felt, he confessed that there was only one thing missing in his life—one thing that his Italian immigrant parents would have wanted him to do—and that was to meet the pope. Well, Phil's revelation caused Yankee owner George Steinbrenner to swing into action, and soon after I received a call from his friend, businessman Bill Fugazy, asking if there was anything I could do. After clearing it with New York's John Cardinal O'Connor, I helped make it happen—and arranged a luncheon for the Rizzutos afterward at my residence in Rome.

The day of the papal audience, the other luncheon guests—a group of American bishops, priests, and embassy staff, all of whom were big Yankees fans—arrived early and we watched a live broadcast of the event on Vatican TV, which included a great shot of Phil and his wife, shaking hands and receiving the blessing of the pope as he made his way down the line. When the Rizzutos arrived at Villa Richardson a half hour later, we sat down in the garden to enjoy our meal. But within minutes, a phone call came for Phil. It was a sports reporter calling from New York who wanted to know how his meeting with the pope had gone. Phil said he'd take the call, and he got up from the table and went into the house, into the Nancy Reagan Sunroom, to talk to the guy. But since the windows were open, those of us in the garden could both see him and hear every word of his end of the conversation. It went something like this:

"Yeah, yeah, it was a big thrill," Phil said, obviously referring to meeting the pope.

"Yeah, he's a *big* baseball fan. He couldn't stop asking questions."

"Oh, like DiMaggio and Williams. He wanted to know who was better. I told him Ted was a better hitter, but Joltin' Joe was a better all-around player. That's why we won all the time." As he was talking, Phil had the phone tucked between his shoulder and his ear and was using both hands to swing an imaginary bat.

Everybody at the table was watching Phil, then looking at one another. One of the guys from my embassy staff looked worried, as if he was afraid Phil might be creating an international incident. A bishop sitting across from me just smiled and shrugged, as if he couldn't believe his ears—but knew it was harmless.

Phil kept right on going. "I told him the ball was definitely more lively today . . . and that if we had been using it, we'd all hit a lot more home runs." He must have been on the phone for fifteen minutes, describing his conversation about baseball with the Holy Father in tremendous detail. The last thing he said was that the pope loved it when he said "Holy Cow!" while broadcasting Yankees games. When he was finally through, he hung up the phone and came back to the table with a satisfied look on his face.

"Phil, that was quite a conversation you claimed to have had with the Holy Father," I said, smiling so he would know that we were all amused by it and nobody was offended. "There's only two problems."

"Like what?" Phil wanted to know, still standing at his place.

"Well, for one thing, I don't think the pope knows that much about baseball."

Phil shrugged as if to say, "Who's to know?"

"The other thing," I said, "is that you only had ten seconds with him. We all watched it, right here on television. You couldn't possibly have talked that much about baseball—or anything—in such a short time."

"It was on TV!" Phil said, surprised. Then he thought a minute and shrugged. "I just hope they don't get that channel back home in New York."

Everyone at the table roared with laughter. The Yankees Hall of Famer sat down, and we finished our meal.

Although there can be lighter moments, most of the time a private audience with the pope is a deeply meaningful experience. Soon after I first got to Rome, I got a phone call from Father James Quigley, O.P., the vice president of Providence College, who told me that he was coming over to Rome soon with a young man named Marty Graham and Marty's parents, Mel and Charlene. I knew Marty because he was a student at Providence College, and a classmate and good friend of my daughter, Julie. He was a handsome boy, a fine Catholic, and a real gentleman. But on the phone that day, Father Quigley told me something about Marty that I hadn't known.

"Marty's got a rare form of bone cancer, Ray," Father Quigley said, "and he doesn't have long to live. He and his parents are devout

Catholics. They don't have a lot of money. But all Marty's friends and the kids at Providence College got together and chipped in to pay for them to take a trip to Rome. Is there any way you could help get him in to see the Holy Father?"

I told Father Quigley that I would try, and called Monsignor Monduzzi, who is in charge of those kind of appointments and who had been very kind to me—despite the fact that I'd snuck in an "extra family member" in my first official meeting with the Holy Father.

"Raymond," Monsignor Monduzzi said in his heavily Italian-accented English, "you have only just arrived and already you are always calling me. How is it you know so many people? I can't get everyone you know inside. Maybe the next ambassador won't have so many friends," he said, laughing.

"Well, Monsignor," I replied, "just listen to this story." I repeated what Father Quigley had told me, but just to be sure he understood, I put my daughter Julie, who by then had learned to speak Italian fluently, on the phone to make sure he understood the situation completely.

When I got back on the phone, Monsignor Monduzzi said, "I'm sorry, but this is a difficult time. His Holiness is very busy. Lech Walesa is coming from Poland. All sorts of leaders are coming from all over the world. I would like to . . . but I don't see how." He promised, though, that if I got him the boy's name, he would ask the pope to pray for him at Mass. I gave Marty's name to Monsignor Monduzzi, but then, two or three days later, I got a phone call from the monsignor.

"Raymond," he said, "you know I was just trying to do my job. But your friend's story is so moving. And when I told the Holy Father, he said to add the family to the special list."

I thanked Monsignor Monduzzi and asked him to thank His Holiness. Then, as soon as I got off the phone with him, I called Father Quigley in Providence to tell him the good news.

When Father Quigley and the Grahams arrived in Rome, I brought them to the Wednesday general audience. As usual, every one of the six thousand seats in the vast Paul VI Hall was filled. I sat with members of the diplomatic corps up front, but Father Quigley and the

Graham family were even closer. They were in the special section of folding chairs set up between the first row of fixed seats and the stage. From where I sat I could see everything that followed.

After the short service and the pope's address, the regular audience ended. Then the pope made his way down the low steps of the stage to greet people. I watched him make his way toward the special section. At one point, he stopped and turned to Monsignor Monduzzi, who was accompanying him, as if to ask him something. I had described the Grahams to the monsignor and told him that Marty would be using crutches, and I saw the monsignor nod toward the young man. As everyone in the hall stood and watched, the Holy Father walked over to Marty who was sitting, staring up at the pope, almost transfixed. When the Holy Father stood before Marty, he put his two hands on the young man's shoulders, leaned over, and rested his forehead against Marty's. Then they prayed together while a Vatican photographer took their picture and Marty's parents, standing on either side of him, looked on with pride, tears streaming down their faces.

Marty died a few months later. The picture of Marty praying with the Holy Father in Rome was displayed next to the young man's casket at his funeral. His parents told me that, as hard as it was to lose him, it was made easier because before he died Marty had the chance to meet John Paul II.

16

HOLY WEEK IN ROME

Can't get enough of these long religious ceremonies

In the spring of 1994 I experienced my first Holy Week in Rome, and although I was awed by the pageantry and tradition of the church's holiest rites, I was even more impressed by the pope's stamina in presiding over all of them—the Holy Thursday service, which commemorates Christ's proclamation of humility to his Apostles; hearing the confessions of ordinary parishioners on Good Friday afternoon; the *Via Crucis* (Way of the Cross) at the Colosseum that evening, which is attended by fifty thousand and is televised to millions around the world; the candlelit Holy Saturday vigil; and Easter Sunday Mass in St. Peter's Square, after which he delivers his *Urbi et Orbi* message. The services are beautiful, but they are long—an American archbishop jokingly calls them "bladder busters." To officiate over them takes not only spiritual strength but physical strength as well.

The Holy Thursday service that year was held at the Church of St. John Lateran, the official cathedral of Rome and the place where popes resided from the fourth century until they returned to Rome after the Avignon "captivity" in France in the fourteenth century. Members of the diplomatic corps were invited, and I was glad to attend. I had never been to "The Lateran" before, and I was stunned by its beauty. Smaller than St. Peter's, the cathedral has its own majesty, with rows of tall, white, marble columns rising to a gold paneled ceiling. Larger-than-life statues of the Apostles line the main aisle, and the altar is topped by a gold-leaf *baldacchino* (four columns topped by a canopy), not as massive as the one in St. Peter's but in its own way just as ornate.

The pope celebrated the Mass assisted by a number of other priests, including Camillo Cardinal Ruini, Vicar General of the Diocese of Rome. Members of the diplomatic corps were seated just to the right of the altar and we were allowed to receive Communion from the Holy Father. After Communion, the pope, dressed in simple white robes, descended from the altar, walked partway down the aisle, knelt, and washed the feet of twelve fellow priests, reenacting what Christ did before the Apostles on the night before he was crucified. Once that part of the ceremony was over, the pope returned to the altar. At the end of the service, the altar cloths were removed and the altar was left bare, in order to prepare for the sadness of Good Friday.

It's a long service, but a beautiful one. After it was over, Kathy and I and some of the other ambassadors and their wives were standing outside the cathedral in the *Piazza di Porta San Giovannia*. We weren't waiting for the Holy Father, but, coincidentally, he came out of a door nearby. Making his way carefully toward his waiting car over the *sampietrini,* the Roman cobblestones, he saw us and took a short detour to come over and say hello.

"We were just talking about the service, Holy Father," I told him. "I was saying how beautiful it was."

"Are you sure you were not complaining at the length?" the Holy Father replied. Everyone laughed. But the Holy Father, not content with one successful joke, decided on adding another. Turning to Steve Falaz, the longtime ambassador from Slovenia, who was standing next to me, the Holy Father nodded in my direction and said, "He's new. Wait until he's been here as long as you—then he won't like these long ones so much." Everyone laughed again.

John Paul had done it again, leading a solemn service on one of the most holy days of the church's year—and a few minutes later cracking everyone up and making us all feel like part of his family.

17

THE *SHOAH* CONCERT

Reaching out—and reaching—our Jewish "elder brothers"

I've already described how I took every opportunity I could to see the pope in action and hear him speak. Once, though, I ran into him when I wasn't trying to.

John Paul II is said to have built a bridge to the Jews. In his first year as pope, he visited the site of the former Auschwitz concentration camp, which is not far from where he grew up in Wadowice. In 1986, he became the first pope to visit and pray in the great Jewish synagogue in Rome. Later, he proclaimed Jews the "elder brothers" of Catholics and issued a pastoral letter condemning anti-Semitism as a sin. In March 2000, in what his spokesman, Dr. Joaquin Navarro-Valls, told me the Holy Father considered "one of the most important pilgrimages of his pontificate," he would make a historical trip to the Holy Land and places sacred to Christians, Muslims, and Jews.

In April 1994, I witnessed another of those gestures of reconciliation when John Paul II held a concert to commemorate the *Shoah*, the attempt to exterminate European Jews, at the Vatican. The invitation to the concert in Paul VI Hall asked everyone to "be in place" at 5:45 P.M. My wife and daughters were there on time, but for some reason I was running late. Rather than go all the way around to the rear entrance that was used by the diplomatic corps, I decided to take a shortcut through the front. The main entrance was closed to the public by the time I arrived, but the Swiss Guards and the plainclothes security people knew me well enough to let me through. When I got inside the lobby, though, I ran into Edward Cardinal Cassidy, the president of the Pontifical Council for Promoting Christian Unity who was in charge of the evening's event, and a small group of people who turned out to be the guests of honor. I tried to duck back out, but Cardinal Cassidy called me over and introduced me to everyone—Italian president Oscar Luigi Scalfro; some members of the Italian senate; Rabbi Elio Toaff, the chief rabbi of Rome, whom I already knew; and some other Jewish leaders.

After the introductions, Cardinal Cassidy thanked me for helping to make some of the arrangements for the concert and asked about some U.S. Church officials who we both knew. Finally, I was able to ask him why they were gathered there. "We're waiting for the pope," he said. It turned out that, for this particular concert, the pope and his guests were going to enter the hall from the rear and walk to armchairs that had been placed halfway down the center aisle. Then it dawned on me—Cardinal Cassidy was under the mistaken impression that I was supposed to be part of his group. But I wasn't—I should have been inside in my seat.

Just then the front doors opened, and the pope entered. The Holy Father's face was beaming. He seemed energized. He immediately rushed up to Rabbi Toaff, embraced him, held him by the shoulders, while the two of them talked animatedly in Italian. It was clear that they had become close friends and that both were excited about the night's event. When the Holy Father and Rabbi Toaff finished their conversation, the pope came around and hugged everyone else—Cardinal Cassidy, President Scalfro and the others, even me, the American ambassador who wasn't really supposed to be there. I had never seen him so excited before. This was obviously a special night for Catholic–Jewish relations and a special night for him.

The papal master of ceremonies came over and started to get everyone in place. Finally, with everyone's attention diverted, I took the opportunity to slip into the auditorium, and make my way down the aisle and to my seat. When I got there, Kathy gave me one of those "Where have you been?" looks. But before I could explain, everyone in the hall stood and turned to watch the Holy Father and the others enter and take their places. The hall was filled to capacity. Many in the audience wore dark clothes and black *yarmulkes*, and I remember thinking Rabbi Toaff must have brought his whole congregation with him and wondering how many of them were inside the Vatican for the first time. The entire diplomatic corps was there. But the most special guests were two hundred Holocaust survivors, many wearing blue-and-white scarves made from the clothing worn by inmates of the death camps.

It was a moving and memorable event. A ten-year-old girl, the daughter of a Holocaust survivor, lit six of the nine candles of the menorah, one for each million Jews killed by the Nazis. Then the Royal Philharmonic Orchestra, conducted by Gilbert Levine, the former conductor of the Kraków Philharmonic Symphony, played the *Kol Nidrei*, the prayer said on Yom Kippur, the Jewish Day of Atonement. Leonard Bernstein's Symphony No. 3, the *Kaddish*, followed, with the prayer read by actor Richard Dreyfuss. By the time the concert was over, most of the audience was crying—Holocaust survivors, cardinals, bishops, even members of the orchestra. It was one of the most extraordinary things I have ever witnessed.

The performance drew long and loud applause. After it was over, the pope rose from his seat, the audience grew quiet, and the Holy Father in a strong, loud voice, proclaimed: "This must not be forgotten!" John Paul went up on the stage then and shook hands with the conductor and all of the featured performers. I looked around me in the audience and saw the Holocaust survivors following his every move. It was clear that even though they practiced a different faith, they believed in this man and they were glad to have been invited into the Vatican. I remembered something my mother used to say: "If you're invited to someone's home, that means they consider you a friend." Through this concert, John Paul II was declaring to the world that Catholics and Jews were friends.

Afterward, there was a reception in the *Sala dei Paramente*, off the *Cortile San Damaso*, the cobblestoned interior courtyard of the Apostolic Palace. The sixteenth-century white marble fountain splashed in the background while Holocaust survivors and members of the synagogue in Rome stood talking with red-hatted cardinals, crimson-wearing bishops, diplomats in tails, and Italian politicians and businessman in dark suits. At one point, Cardinal Cassidy approached me and asked, "Where did you go?"

I told him that I wasn't supposed to be in his group in the first place and said, "You almost got me in trouble with the pope."

"Oh, don't worry," Cardinal Cassidy said, laughing. "You know he couldn't care less about all that protocol business. Besides, did you see him? He was shining all night. This was a great night for him, something that meant a lot to him, a dream of his. I've never seen him so happy."

Later, Richard Dreyfuss and I talked with some Italian Jews who were describing what Rome was like during the war. As one of the elderly people said, "Much hurt, but now much joy."

The next night, at a dinner party hosted by *New York Times* reporter John Tagliabue, Gilbert Levine told all of us how wonderful the concert had been. But what had been even more special, he said, was the previous day's meeting between the pope and Holocaust survivors, including Levine's mother-in-law. "He was incredible! Awesome, really, with each one of them!" Levine told us. "And my mother-in-law, you can't imagine what it was like for her! When her turn came, it was as if they were the only two people in the room. There they were, going on and on in Polish. And the great thing was, he showed her that he knew, that he understood, what she and the others had gone through. That's what meant so much to my mother-in-law. To have the pope . . . this pope . . . say 'I know, I understand' to someone who suffered so much. It gave a meaning to the suffering that helped ease the pain."

18

THE CAIRO CONFERENCE

Fighting a war for life

So far, all my encounters with John Paul II had been very positive. During much of 1994, however, I was forced to see him under much different—and more tense—circumstances. It was during that time that he fought his year-long battle against what he saw as threats to the sanctity of life—threats backed by the Clinton administration—that were raised as part of the United Nations Conference for Population and Development held in Cairo that September.

The Cairo conference was the third in a series of U.N. conferences in ten-year intervals. As their title suggests, these conferences were supposed to deal with both population *and* development. The two earlier conferences had put most of their emphasis on the development side. Much of the discussion centered around steps that poorer countries could take to improve their standard of living—through investments in infrastructure, education, and so on. Population control advocates had actually suffered a severe setback in the 1984 conference in Mexico City, when the U.S. government, always the key player in these conferences, cut all support for family planning and population control under orders from President Reagan. At the Cairo Conference, though, population control zealots were desperately trying to make a comeback. They were pushing a radical plan to nearly triple the amount of money spent on population control—from $6 billion to $17 billion by the year 2000—and to promote abortion as a method of family planning. The draft of the proposed conference report—circulated for comments during the previous year—contained language such as:

> All countries should strive to make accessible through the primary health care systems reproductive health to all individuals . . . primary health care should include . . . pregnancy termination.

Religious and political leaders all over the world, especially those from developing countries, opposed this plan. They argued that the First World had created the population problem but was trying to make the Third World solve it. They even accused the U.N. and the U.S. of engaging in "reproductive blackmail," since it was being proposed that economic development aid be conditional, based on the success of population control efforts. But, as with every major moral issue in the last twenty years of the century, it was John Paul II who led the fight.

Despite the opposition, even by the pope, the population control plan seemed destined to prevail, because its advocates now had a friend in the White House. Candidate Bill Clinton had downplayed abortion during his presidential election campaign, trying to portray himself as a moderate on the issue. The only time he talked specifically about abortion was at a speech he gave at the University of Notre Dame, an event to which I accompanied him, where he said he wanted to make abortion "safe, legal, and rare." Upon taking office, though, Clinton proved to be anything but moderate. Immediately, his administration loosened federal restrictions on abortion, doubled U.S. support for family planning, and appointed Joycelyn Elders, who was radically pro-choice, as surgeon general. This put me in a tough spot. When I took the job as ambassador to the Holy See, I thought I could help provide some balance to the liberals who had captured the Clinton-Gore administration in its early going and help build a positive relationship between the White House and the Vatican. As the Cairo debate unfolded, I realized I'd been a bit naive to think that. I found myself between a rock and a hard place, representing the Clinton administration on the one hand but agreeing with John Paul II on the other.

John Paul II wasn't naive, however. Early on, he blasted the proposed Cairo plan as a "serious setback for humanity" and "a United Nations plan to destroy the family." He also used every weapon in his arsenal to defeat it. Before the year started, he designated 1994 the "Year of the Family." In early February, he released a "Letter to Families," and he had *L'Osservatore Romano,* the official daily newspaper of the Vatican, devote nine pages to it. The gist of the letter was that government should be promoting, not undermining, the family as way to make the world a better place to live. John Paul II used every opportunity to speak out against the proposed Cairo plan—including his Sunday Angelus message and his weekly addresses to his general audience. But it wasn't only *what* he said, it was the *way* he said it. His voice rose. He turned red in the face. He clenched his fist and shook it in righteous indignation. "We protest!" he shouted once from his window to the crowds gathered below in St. Peter's Square. He even used the canonization of a modern saint to deliver his message, beatifying Dr. Gianna Beretta Molla, a pregnant pediatrician, who died in 1962, after she chose life for her baby over life for herself when complications arose during the delivery operation.

In April, the pope sent a personally signed letter to every head of state in the world and to the secretary-general of the U.N. denouncing the Cairo proposal for promoting a "society of things and not of persons," and declaring that "what threatens the family threatens mankind." I was summoned to the Vatican by Archbishop Tauran to personally receive the letter which I was forwarding directly to President Clinton. It was an unusual meeting. Generally, Archbishop Tauran began a meeting by making small talk. He'd ask about my family or talk about the last opera he'd attended, because he knew I was also an opera fan. In fact, I'd just seen *Aida* at Rome's ancient outdoor theater, the *Caracalla,* and I looked forward to telling him about it. But when I walked into his office, Tauran was all business. "The Holy Father wants your president to receive this," was all that he said. It was the shortest meeting I'd ever attended.

A week later, the pope called the ambassadors of all the countries with diplomatic relations with the Vatican—over 150 of us—into the

Sala Regia, one of the most ornate rooms in the Vatican. Not only did the Holy Father proceed to blast the Cairo proposal, but he brought in all the "heavy hitters" in the Curia to do the same—Cardinal Secretary of State Angelo Sodano; Secretary for Relations with States Jean-Louis Tauran; Roger Cardinal Etchegaray, head of the Pontifical Council for Justice and Peace; and Alfonso Cardinal Lopez Trujillo, head of the Pontifical Council for the Family. It was like having the president deliver a message to joint session of Congress—and then having all his cabinet secretaries get up and reinforce it. After the briefing, which was more like a tongue-lashing, all of the ambassadors lined up as usual for a few words with the Holy Father. Usually, I looked forward to the opportunity. This time, I dreaded it. Everybody in the room knew that the United States was the driving force behind Cairo, and I felt they were all watching to see what happened when it was my turn. When I finally stepped before the Holy Father, he took my hands in his, looked me right in the eye, and said, "Your government *must not* allow this!"

John Paul II can be very kind, friendly, and engaging. But that day he was as forceful and direct as I'd ever seen him. I wanted to thank him for his moral courage and his willingness to take on this fight. I wanted to tell him I agreed with him. Of course I couldn't, because I was representing "the other side." All I could say in response was, "Your Holiness, I understand."

The pope took a lot of heat for the relentless nature of his campaign. Some people couldn't understand why he kept it up, day after day. They said he was beginning to sound harsh and reactionary. Liberals—both within and outside the church—called him a "one-issue pope," "anti-woman," "old-fashioned," and "out of touch." The media blasted him, especially the U.S., British, and French, ridiculing his position. Newspaper headlines read: POPE GOES TO WAR AGAINST U.N. ABORTION PROPOSALS. The issue was being portrayed as a fight between millions of young, liberated women in the United States and other parts of the world and a handful of old, repressed men at the Vatican.

I gave the Holy Father all the credit in the world for what he was doing, though. In addition to agreeing with him on the issues, I appreciated what he was putting himself through. You have to have been in politics to understand what it takes to go that far out on a limb for something you believe in, especially when it's not popular and when there's a good chance your position might not prevail. You also have to have been in politics to understand that you don't convince people about an issue—especially one as emotionally charged as abortion—just by making a persuasive argument once and then calling it a day and going home. You do it by going out every day, over and over and over again, and forcing people—and the media—to listen to you whether they want to or not. You don't convince people through persuasiveness but through persistance. That's what the pope was attempting to do on Cairo, and I admired him for it.

But I could tell the pope was feeling the heat. I saw the strain in his face when he hit that section in his speeches that dealt with Cairo. I knew that he knew what the media was saying about him, that he understood his vulnerability to criticism, and that the other side was winning the public relations war. One of the reasons for that was that the pope was almost all by himself on the issue. Other church leaders weren't speaking out nearly as forcefully. In politics, it's nice to have company when you take on tough issues. It's nice not to be the only target, especially when your opposition has the active support of ideological friends in the media. The pope wasn't receiving that kind of backup support, though. There were even some people inside the church who were complaining that he'd gone too far this time. Knowing all that, the pope tried to demonstrate another side of himself and of the Catholic Church. I could see it in the way he used every opportunity to meet and surround himself with women and women's groups. He knew he was vulnerable when it came to so-called women's issues, so he tried to show, as often and as publicly as he could, how much he respected women and the important role women played in the world.

Another way I could tell the pope was feeling the heat was that he let his press secretary, Dr. Joaquin Navarro-Valls, defend him. In an op-ed column in the *Wall Street Journal,* Navarro-Valls wrote: "The Holy Father has spoken a good deal about courage. . . . He means the courage needed by the pope and his bishops to face ridicule and ostracism for their positions on the issues that lie at the foundation of human life and of the Christian revelation. . . . We live in a dishonest age," Navarro-Valls continued. "We call abortion everything but what it is. The Holy Father cuts through that verbiage and calls it an evil as heinous as killing any other human being. This blunt talk sends a shock wave through the highest ranks of our civil societies because many of them have been busy, by their laws, killing our kind and calling it something else." The Holy Father wasn't pulling his punches when it came to the Cairo conference—or calling things by anything but their proper name.

John Paul II's campaign against the Cairo proposal prompted the U.S. government to intensify its own campaign in support of the plan. In March, the State Department sent a directive to all U.S. embassies explaining the "party line" as far as Cairo was concerned. The memo said, in part: ". . . the United States believes access to safe, legal and voluntary abortion is a fundamental right of all women." The memo was followed by phone calls to all the U.S. embassies reiterating the U.S. position.

A few weeks later, I was called to Washington to receive a briefing on the plan by the Clinton administration's "point person" on the Cairo conference, Assistant Secretary of State for Global Affairs Tim Wirth, and his staff. I knew Wirth from his days as a liberal Democratic U.S. senator from Colorado. I also knew that he thought population growth was the single most serious threat the world faced today and that he was so gung ho on the issue that he had a "condom tree" prominently displayed in his office at the State Department. I wasn't surprised, then, when my briefing turned into an hour-long lecture on why the U.S. policy was so obviously the correct one and how the pope and the Catholic Church just "didn't get it." I took offense when Wirth said to me, "This isn't a religious issue. It's a political issue. And we've got to move on."

"You're wrong," I told him. "This *is* a religious issue. It *is* a moral issue. But you're right that it's also a political issue. The trouble is—it's not only bad policy, it's bad politics." Then I told him that it didn't make sense for the Clinton administration to alienate the Catholic Church if it wanted to do anything on health care and welfare reform.

While I said it, I thought to myself: I thought it was supposed to be "the economy, stupid," not "the condoms, stupid."

But Secretary Wirth didn't want to hear what I had to say, not then, not later. Before our meeting, I was supposed to be a member of the U.S. delegation to the Cairo Conference. After it, my name was taken off the list.

After striking out with Wirth, I made one more attempt to get somebody at the State Department to understand the pope's concerns. I went to New York and met with then-U.N. Ambassador Madeleine Albright and told her how seriously the pope was taking the Cairo conference. But either she wasn't interested or I wasn't very persuasive. In case it was the second possibility, I asked Albright if she'd stop in and let John Cardinal O'Connor, Archbishop of New York, talk to her about Cairo. O'Connor was leading the fight against the Cairo plan in the United States, and I knew from talking with him that he'd welcome a chance to meet with Ambassador Albright, as he'd met with her predecessors, something that was fairly easy to do since the U.N. is right around the corner from the archbishop's residence in Manhattan. Ambassador Albright promised she would call on the cardinal, but the next time I saw her and asked how it went, she admitted that she'd been too busy to do it.

In April, the pope decided to take his fight directly to the president— and he asked me to help him. One Friday afternoon, I received a call from Archbishop Jean-Louis Tauran, Secretary for Relations with States. Archbishop Tauran didn't call often, so when he did I knew something was up—something important. He asked me if I would come to his office the next morning. He apologized for the short notice and for the Saturday appointment, but said that it was urgent we meet. He didn't tell me what he wanted to talk about, but I suspected it was Cairo. An hour later, he called back and confirmed my hunch. "I'm with the Holy Father," Archbishop Tauran said. "He does not want his message misunderstood. The reason I need to speak with you tomorrow has to do with the Cairo conference." He didn't say it was "important" this time—but that was hardly necessary. Two calls in an hour! The pope standing next to him! Our meeting was obviously top priority.

The next morning, I met with Archbishop Tauran in his office. He is an extremely intelligent and serious man, but also very gracious. Kathy and I had gotten to know him very well thanks to a series of luncheons that William Cardinal Baum had arranged when we first arrived in Rome. After asking after my wife and family, Archbishop Tauran got down to business. "This meeting in Cairo and the document that is being drawn up are very important to the church," he said, "so important that the Holy Father would like to talk with your president. He would like to arrange to have a telephone conversation with him as soon as it would be convenient."

Archbishop Tauran stood up then, stepped away from his desk, and motioned for me to follow him. We walked out of his office; past one set of Swiss Guards; down the third-floor hallway of the Apostolic Palace which is lined with ancient maps on tapestries along the walls and frescoes on the ceilings; and then went around the corner of the U-shaped corridor to the other wing of the building, past another set of Swiss Guards, to where the pope's private quarters are located. This was very unusual. In Washington, it would be like meeting with the Speaker of the House of Representatives and then having him walk you from the Capitol to the White House to go see the president.

When we got to the doorway of the pope's library, we paused for a minute. The Holy Father was inside talking with some people. When they left, we entered the room. The Holy Father greeted me warmly, then stepped back and looked at me seriously. "Ambassador," he said, "I think it is necessary that I talk to your president. I know he is very busy, but I want to talk to him about something that is very important to the church and to all society. We must be a world that values and protects and respects all life. I look forward to talking to him about that. Tell him I pray for his family and for the wonderful people of your great nation."

That was it; the meeting was over. The pope thanked me for coming, then turned and walked over to greet another group that had just come in. But I understood why this had all been stage-managed the way it had. John Paul II is very sophisticated politically. He knew that if I told the White House that his request to talk to the president had been relayed to me by another Vatican official—even one as important as Archbishop Tauran—the request wouldn't be taken as seriously as if I could say it came directly from the pope himself. He figured that would help guarantee that the call would happen. Little did he know—or I know—how hard it would be to arrange.

Archbishop Tauran walked me back to the elevator. He told me the pope understood that, because it was a weekend and because of the time difference, it might be difficult for the president to call that day. If he did, though, Archbishop Tauran said that the pope would be available to take the call until ten P.M., Rome time, and all afternoon and all evening the next day. I left the Apostolic Palace, returned to my residence, and immediately called the White House, and relayed the pope's request. Because it was a Saturday, no one from the regular White House staff was around. For something as important as this, I didn't think that would be a problem. Just to make sure, I called back a few hours later and left the same message a second time.

On Sunday morning, I called the Vatican to find out if a call had been received from the White House the night before. I was told that it had not. It was too early in the U.S. for me to call Washington again, so at noon Kathy and I went over to St. Peter's to hear the pope deliver his Angelus message to the crowd gathered in the square. Once again the pope talked forcefully about the need to promote a "culture of life" and the obligation of Catholics to defend life everywhere. That afternoon, I called the White House, but nobody could tell me anything about the phone call and nobody with any clout was around. Evidently, people in the Clinton administration took their weekends seriously.

I was getting annoyed. The delay was an insult to the pope and a poor reflection on the president—and it wasn't very good for me, either. Being able to deliver on a request like this is what gives an ambassador credibility. The pope is a special person and the Vatican is a special place, but in matters like this, things operate as they do anywhere else. People in authority want to deal with those who have the "juice" to get things done. So far, on this assignment, I wasn't measuring up.

On Monday, around noon, Rome time, I finally got through to Mac McLarty, the president's chief of staff, and someone everybody credits with being a real pro and a straight shooter. Mac told me that he'd been out of town for the weekend and had just gotten in. He said that he hadn't heard anything about the phone call, and that he'd look into it and get back to me. But the rest of the day passed without my receiving a call from the White House—or the Holy Father's getting a call from the president.

I had been frustrated before; now I was angry. Initially, I figured the request for the call might not have gotten through to the president because of some kind of incompetence on the part of the White House staff. Now I wondered if maybe the request wasn't being allowed through because some people just didn't want him to talk to the pope.

By Tuesday morning, I'd had enough. I got on a plane, flew to Washington, and went directly from the airport to the White House. I walked into the Executive Office and told the president's secretary, Betty Currie, that even though I didn't have an appointment I needed to see her boss—and that I'd wait for as long as it took. This was a real roll of the dice on my part. I wasn't sure the president would see me. I didn't know, for sure, if the pope's request was being stonewalled by his staff or if the president himself was doing the stonewalling. I had plenty of time to think about all the possibilities while I waited in the White House reception area, drinking coffee and eating bag after bag of the M&Ms that were set out in bowls for visitors.

I waited all day and didn't get in to see the president. So I came back the next day at eight A.M. to try again. At one point, I called Archbishop Tauran at the Vatican to let him know where I was. I hoped he would tell me that the call had been made, but he didn't. Without actually lying, I tried to make excuses for President Clinton. I said he was having a difficult couple of days and mentioned some issues that were in the news. But I knew—and I knew Archbishop Tauran knew—that *nobody*, not even the president of the United States, could be too busy to talk to the pope.

At one point, I decided to try to see if I'd have better luck getting in to see the vice president. I walked through the passageway into the executive office building and, although I didn't get to see Vice President Gore, I did see one of his top aides, Leon Feurth. I told him about John Paul II's request for a phone call from the president and told him that I thought the administration needed to show consider-

Karol Wojtyla, when he was Cardinal Archbishop of Krakow, on his first visit to Boston in 1969. He stands in front of a monument for Revolutionary War General Kosciusko with Polish and American church leaders, along with State Auditor Ted Buczko (fifth from right) and Deputy Mayor of Boston Ed Sullivan (sixth from right).

While I was mayor of Boston, I had a long discussion with Ronald Reagan about the important role Pope John Paul II had in bringing down Communism.

My visit to the Vatican while mayor of Boston, 1984. A mayor must work for social justice is what the pope told me. *L'OSSERVATORE ROMANO* PHOTO SERVICE

Vice President Al Gore at my swearing in as U.S. Ambassador to the Vatican at the State Department, 1993. My family, from left to right: Kathy, Maureen, Julie, Ray Jr., Katie, Nancy, and Eddie.

Presenting my credentials to the Holy Father Pope John Paul II in 1993. *L'OSSERVATORE ROMANO* PHOTO SERVICE

The Pope, President Bill Clinton, and I at World Youth Day, Denver, August 1993.

Here I am with Pope John Paul II on the way back from Denver, from World Youth Day. "I've seen the youth of America and your country's future is bright," said the pope. *L'OSSERVATORE ROMANO* PHOTO SERVICE

My conversation at the White House when I urged the President to call the pope. Just before the Cairo conference, April 1994.

Greeting the pope at The Vatican with Secretary of State Warren Christopher and President Clinton. Background, left to right: Vatican Secretary of State Angelo Cardinal Sodano and Mrs. Rodham. June 1994.

The Holy Father always expresses interest in family. Left to right: Maureen, Ray Jr., Kathy, me, Pope John Paul II, Ed, Julie, Nancy, and Katie. Christmas, The Vatican, 1995.

The pope's arrival in Newark. On this occasion he asked if we were on schedule. He didn't want to delay Jewish people celebrating their holy days. October 1995.

This photo is from a typical diplomatic function at the Vatican. A warm personal friendship, but sometimes U.S. government policies and the pope's views clashed. (1996)
L'OSSERVATORE ROMANO PHOTO SERVICE

John Cardinal O'Connor always talked about Ray Jr. to the pope when Ray was sick. From left to right: Kathy, Ray Jr., Cardinal O'Connor, and me. U.S. Ambassador's residence in Rome, 1997.

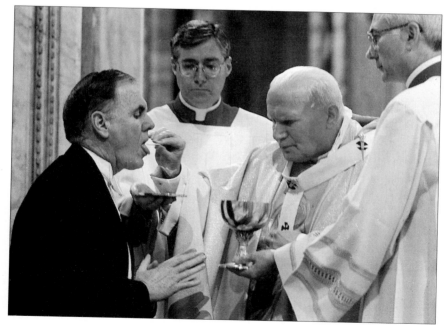

Receiving holy communion from the pope. I had many opportunities to be in the Holy Father's presence during the year. St. John Lateran (Rome), 1996. *L'OSSERVATORE ROMANO*

This is Francis Cardinal Arinze of Nigeria, who is often mentioned as possibly the first modern black pope. Arinze is the Church's leading spokesperson on religious dialogue throughout the world.
Next to him and behind stands one of the most important Vatican officials, Bishop James Harvey, who coordinates the Holy Father's schedule. At my residence in Rome, 1997.

This photo was taken in 1999, in St. Louis, Missouri, where we had a serious discussion about the death penalty.

ation to the leader of the world's one billion Catholics. I don't know whether he passed my concerns on to his boss or not.

Finally, near the end of the second day of my one-man sit-in, I was called into the White House Situation Room, the bunkerlike room with maps on the walls that is used in national security emergencies. Several top White House aides were already there, including Mac McLarty, the president's chief of staff; Sandy Berger, assistant national security advisor; Nancy Soderberg, from the National Security Council; White House Communications Director Mark Gearan; and Susan Brophy, in charge of legislation for the White House. The "meeting" was chaired by my old pal, Assistant Secretary of State Tim Wirth. Wirth got right to the point. "Ambassador Flynn," he said, "a lot of countries have concerns about the Cairo conference and the draft document. But the president has left it up to me and my staff to negotiate with the other countries. Nobody is getting a chance to lobby the president on this one."

"With all due respect," I said to Secretary Wirth, which in this case was code for the exact opposite, "the pope isn't asking to 'lobby' the president. He wants to speak with him."

"There are over one hundred and fifty countries coming to the conference," Wirth replied. "We can't have the president calling up everybody. He can't talk to every head of state."

"The pope isn't just *any* head of state," I told Wirth. "He's the leader of *one billion* Catholics around the world—and over *sixty million* in the United States. I think the president *should* make the call, and I came here to tell him so."

It was quite a scene. The room was silent. I had the feeling that most of the people in it were probably on my side, but since it was Wirth's issue, they felt they had to defer to him. While we were sitting there, national security advisor Tony Lake walked in and took a seat in the back. People were looking at the floor, up at the ceiling, not knowing what to do or say. Finally, Mark Gearan, a veteran of Massachusetts and national Democratic politics, spoke up. "How about this," he said. "Can't we finesse this thing a little bit? Can't we just have the president call the pope as a courtesy. It doesn't *just* have to be about Cairo. They can talk about anything. The president's going to Rome in June. We can say he just called to say he's looking forward to seeing the pope then." Mark was playing the diplomat, and he was doing a good job. I wasn't surprised, later, when he was named to run the Peace Corps. "Whatta ya think, Ray?" he asked me.

"You can say they talked about anything you want," I said. "I don't care if you say they talked about the Red Sox. I just want him to make the phone call."

The tension eased a little. Tony Lake, who hadn't said anything until then, spoke up. "Maybe they *should* talk about the Red Sox," he said. "They need a miracle—and more pitching—if they're ever gonna win the World Series again." That brought laughs and helped everyone relax. Finally, reluctantly, Wirth agreed to Gearan's compromise. I was allowed in to see President Clinton. When I brought up the matter of the phone call, he acted as if it was the first time he'd heard of the pope's request.

"I'd love to talk to him," the president said, I think, genuinely. Because of the time difference he couldn't do it then, but the president called the pope the next day.

I don't know exactly what the pope and the president said to each other during their telephone conversation. I do know that the conversation didn't resolve anything. The United States continued to back the Cairo proposals, which included what was euphemistically described as "pregnancy termination" as a means of population control. The pope continued his opposition. John Paul II's next move was to get the American church more deeply involved in his "culture of life, not death" campaign. Six American cardinals and the president of the U.S. Catholic Bishops' Conference sent a letter to the White House. "However cleverly the current Cairo document may be crafted, in fact it continues to advocate abortion as a way of controlling population growth and promiscuity," they wrote. Then they used the president's own words against him: "As you have stated, Mr. President, 'families raise children, not government.'" They asked him to "shun the advice of those who would apply pressure on developing nations to mandate abortion as a condition for receiving aid from other countries. Do not allow our country to participate in trampling the rights and religious values of people around the world." A month later, the entire membership of the U.S. Bishops Conference sent a similar letter. This one expressed their outrage "that our government is leading the effort to foster global acceptance of abortion."

The only thing that temporarily slowed the Holy Father's campaign occurred a week later, when he fell and broke his femur and had to have an artificial hip implanted. That kept him in the hospital for most of the month of May. But he even used his accident and his injury to reinforce his campaign. In the first Angelus message he delivered after getting out of the hospital, John Paul asked the crowd why he'd had to suffer—and then answered his own question. "Why now, why this, why in this Year of the Family? Precisely because the family is under attack. The pope has to be attacked, the pope has to suffer, so that every family and the world may see that there is, I would say, a higher Gospel: the Gospel of suffering, by which the future is prepared, the third millennium of families, of every family and of all families. . . . Understand it, understand why the pope was in hospital again, suffering again: understand it, think it over!"

As I stood in the crowd at St. Peter's, I overheard a man from California say to his wife: "The pope might be down, but he's not out. There's still a lot of life in him yet."

With the fight over Cairo continuing to rage, June 1994 was not a very good time for President Clinton to meet with John Paul II. But since the president was coming to Rome to celebrate the fiftieth anniversary of the end of World War II, a meeting had to be held. I had a ringside seat for the event, which was being "played" very differently by the opposing sides. The White House tried to downplay the seriousness of the two leaders' meetings and made every effort to avoid mention of the Cairo conference. The pope took the exact opposite approach, and on the day of the meeting, he made sure that *L'Osservatore Romano* ran an editorial on the Cairo conference. The editorial said that the conference needed to approach the issues before it "in a deeply ethical way because they concern the right and dignity of the human being and of the family and the sovereign rights of developing nations." It also reminded everyone—including the visiting

U.S. president—that there were different kinds of imperialism, including "anti-conception imperialism."

As an illustration of how things had changed in U.S.–Vatican relations, whereas in Denver in 1993 I'd been given ample time to brief the president before his meeting with the pope, in Rome, in 1994, I was kept away from him. Protocol demanded that I introduce the two leaders, though, so I used my short time with the president—pausing at the bronze doors and while walking up the steps of the Apostolic Palace—to say, "The pope's not letting up on this Cairo thing. I hope you've got some kind of an answer ready because he *is* going to bring it up."

Inside the Vatican, I introduced the president to the Holy Father, then watched the two leaders walk into the San Rafael room for their private meeting. When they came out a half hour later, I could tell from their body language that things hadn't gone well. The pope wore a stony expression on his face. The president looked a little stunned— a Scripps-Howard reporter described him as "tongue-tied." The usual joint statements were not issued, only a brief ceremony at which gifts were exchanged was held. The pope gave the president, Mrs. Clinton, Mrs. Clinton's mother, Mrs. Rodham, and secretary of state Warren Christopher pewter medallions marking his fifteen years as pope. The president gave the pope a framed mosaic of the Colosseum. When the gift-giving ceremony was over, I walked over to the Holy Father. At first, he looked relieved to see a familiar face. But when I reached his side, he turned to me with a very somber expression and said, "Mr. Ambassador, how did it get this way?"

Afterward, the president tried to put a happy face on things, describing the meeting as "a wonderful discussion" to a group of Americans living in Rome and seminarians from the North American College gathered in the *Sala Clementina*. But the pope didn't pretend—or halt his offensive. A few days later, an extraordinary consistory in Rome, the world's cardinals released a statement saying that "the family should be free of coercion, particularly in regard to the question of procreation" and the "failed social policies of many developed nations should not be foisted on the world's poor." And the pope kept up his campaign in a series of speeches over the rest of the summer, ripping the proposed Cairo plan as "a danger for all humanity" and a violation of married couples' "basic human rights."

On June 29, in his first public ceremony since his hip operation, the pope celebrated a Mass in honor of Saints Peter and Paul in St. Peter's Basilica. Members of the diplomatic corps were invited, and we were all sitting in our usual places. Sometimes, the grandeur of the place, the height of the dome, and the bronze canopy supported by twisted black-and-gold columns that tower over the altar makes it hard to concentrate on what is being said or done there. But this wasn't one of those times. Everyone was watching the Holy Father even more intently than usual, trying to judge his health and wondering what he would do or say next about Cairo.

When it came time for the homily, the pope sat in the throne a few feet away from the altar. A priest set up a small, goosenecked microphone next to the chair, and the pope's secretary, Monsignor Vincent Tran Ngoc Thu, handed the pope the text of his speech. John Paul read it, word for word. He spoke about Christ's calling Peter the "rock" upon which he would built His church and Paul His "chosen instrument" to spread his name to all people on earth. But then the Holy Father stopped and looked up from his papers. The Holy Father seldom departs from his prepared text: all of us in the diplomatic corps knew that. But now he did, and all the ambassadors leaned forward in their seats to listen. I was sitting in the first row, next to Steve Falaz, the ambassador to the Vatican from Slovenia and someone with over forty years of experience in Rome. Steve nudged me with his elbow as if to say "Pay attention."

Suddenly, the Holy Father's voice was louder and more forceful. He became more animated, he sat straighter in his chair. He wasn't talking about Saints Peter and Paul anymore, but about the threat to the sanctity of life posed by the Cairo conference. It was so quiet in St. Peter's that you could hear a pin drop. After Mass, as we were leaving, the French ambassador came up behind me. "Nothing stops him," he said. "He just won't quit." The ambassador for Germany summed it up: "You're either with him or against him on this one. There is no in between." He's right, I thought to myself, on something like this, there's no purgatory, there's only heaven or hell. But then I thought of my own situation. I was with the Holy Father on the issue, but I was representing the United States, which was on the other side. If there was no in between, where did that put me? Between a rock and a hard place, I guessed.

With only a few months to go until the conference, the pope really shook things up. Until then, he had been fighting pretty much single-handedly. The pro–population control forces counted on that and figured he would have only a handful of delegates from Catholic countries on his side when the conference convened. The pope knew that, so he did what every good campaigner does—he recruited new allies to join him in his fight, and they came from what might have seemed an unlikely area—nations in the Islamic world.

The pope dispatched Archbishop Tauran and other church officials to talk to religious and political leaders in various Arab countries, including Libya and Iran, and they responded by joining him in denouncing the Cairo plan. In mid-August, Saudi Arabia announced that it would boycott the Cairo conference in protest. Sudan and Lebanon soon followed suit, and although delegations from their countries still planned to attend, several prominent female Muslim leaders, including Prime Minister Tansu Ciller of Turkey, Prime Minister Khaleda Zia of Bangladesh, and Queen Noor of Jordan announced that they would boycott Cairo, too. Highly respected scholars at Al Azhar University and the American Muslim Council denounced the proposed Cairo document with language that sounded almost exactly like that used by the pope. Mohammed Salahideen, a leading Islamic columnist, wrote: "This is an attempt to tear the values and beliefs of Islam from their roots. It is a ferocious attack on Islam and Muslims and their most holy beliefs."

This seemed to finally get the attention of the Clinton administration. First, it tried to paint these Muslim countries as a bunch of religious fanatics who were anti-women. When that didn't work, and it seemed more and more that the United States was trying to dictate its secular policies to religious nations, the administration tried to backpedal. In August, Vice President Al Gore tried to deny that the United States was promoting abortion, saying during a speech to the

National Press Club: "The United States has not sought, does not seek, and will not seek to establish an international right to abortion. This is a red herring."

But the pope wouldn't let Vice President Gore get away with this denial. A few days later, the pope's official spokesperson, Papal Press Secretary Joaquin Navarro-Valls, who never makes a statement without the pope's blessing, responded: "The draft population document, which has the United States as its principal sponsor, contradicts, in reality, Mr. Gore's statement." In plain English, rather than diplomatic-speak, he called the vice president a liar. It doesn't get much worse than that in international relations. When I saw Navarro-Valls recently in Rome and reminded him of the incident, he laughed—but he didn't apologize. "Those were the facts," he said to me.

At the beginning of September, the nine-day Cairo Conference finally convened with over 15,000 delegates from 185 countries attending. U.S. Assistant Secretary Tim Wirth attempted to ignore the pope's ferocious and very public campaign and tried to put a ridiculously positive spin on the proceedings, announcing: "I cannot remember an international conference with such very broad agreement at the beginning. Those who are unhappy with it are a very small minority." But it wasn't true. Prime Minister Benazir Bhutto of Pakistan said: "The world needs consensus. It does not need a clash of cultures. Where there is no consensus there will have to be a willing, whole-hearted recognition and acceptance of diversity. . . . Regrettably, this conference's document contains serious flaws striking at the heart of a great many cultural values in the north and in the south and in the church and in the mosque."

Delegates wrangled for days over the wording of the 113-page final report, "A Program of Action." Debate was especially heated over paragraph 8.25, which promoted abortion as a fundamental right for all women. When Vatican representatives tried to object to it, they were booed. The conference chairman Dr. Fred Sal, did nothing to stop the booing, either, letting it build, in an obvious effort to embarrass the Catholic Church. This was hardly surprising, since he happened to be president of the International Planned Parenthood Association.

When it came time to produce the final document, the Vatican and its allies succeeded in inserting a statement that said: "In no case should abortion be promoted as a method of family planning." That was enough to prompt *Time* magazine to declare: "In the end, the pope won."

But I don't think anybody won at Cairo. I think everyone lost.

Certainly the poor countries of the world lost. The debate over population control took so long that there was no time left to talk about development. When Vatican representatives called on the United States and other developed nations to increase aid to Third World development efforts, the motion was rejected—a move in which, according to *L'Osservatore Romano,* "rich countries revealed their greed."

The United States lost at Cairo. It came away looking like a bully, like it was trying to steamroll its view that abortion was a legitimate tool for population control—despite the objections of countries and religions around the world. Internationally, the Clinton administration displayed either an unwillingness or an inability to show respect and understanding for the religious values that inform public policy everywhere else in the world. Politically, I *thought* the Clinton administration lost big-time by alienating the pope and the Catholic Church just to please what amounted to a small, but vocal, minority of liberal and feminist groups. A few years later, though, I was proved wrong. Because it was just those groups who kept President Clinton in office after he was impeached over the Monica Lewinsky scandal.

I lost a lot over Cairo. My relationships with the president, the White House, and the State Department were never the same afterward. But I did learn something, and it was John Paul II who taught it to me. I've always thought of politics as the art of compromise, and I always prided myself on being able to bring people together, even over issues that divided them. During the Cairo controversy, though, the pope showed me that sometimes—when morality is at stake—there can be no compromise, no way to bring people together. All you can to is to try to persuade them to do what's right and pray for them if they don't.

John Paul II won my respect and that of a lot of other people for fighting the good fight over the Cairo conference. In Boston, we have an expression: "Everybody wants to go to heaven, but nobody wants to die." Well, the pope wasn't afraid to die fighting against the "culture of death." *Time* magazine named him its "Man of the Year" for 1994, a year which the magazine described as "when so many people lamented the decline of moral values or made excuses for bad behavior." In an interview, the Holy Father told *Time*: "The pope must be a moral force," and he made a clear distinction between what's popular and what's right. "It is a mistake to apply American democratic procedures to the faith and the truth," the pope said. "You cannot take a vote on the truth. You must not confuse the *sensus fidei* (sense of the faith) with consensus."

John Paul II's image suffered greatly. Thanks to the way the other side positioned him and the way their friends in the media—the liberal Western media, anyway—portrayed him, the pope came away from Cairo looking harsh, old-fashioned, and out of touch—and seeming to be against women, modernism, and progress. It wasn't true, of course, but, unlike John Paul II, the media doesn't always present us with the truth.

19

EVEN THE POPE SOMETIMES FEELS THE BURDEN

Sensing a melancholy pope

One of the best-kept secrets in Rome was the rosary service the pope led on the first Saturday of every month. Although it was sometimes held on a large scale in Paul VI Hall, usually it was an intimate service, held in a small room in the Apostolic Palace. Sometimes as few as thirty or forty people were invited. People who did know about it and had somehow managed to get their names on the guest list would wait at the Bronze Doors at seven P.M. Then the Swiss Guards, after checking to make sure they were on the list, would let them in. Visiting dignitaries and celebrities never attended and I never saw anyone else from the diplomatic corps.

Dr. Marjorie Weeke, who works for the Pontifical Council for Social Communications, was in charge of the service, and she really liked Kathy, so whenever she could she'd get us in. We both loved the service, it reminded us of Wednesday novenas back home at Mission Church and of saying the rosary along with Cardinal Cushing on the radio when we were kids.

The Holy Father liked the service, too, because it was intimate and because people didn't come to see him so much as to pray with him. The pope would enter the room, dressed plainly in his white, caped cassock and white skullcap, proceed over to the kneeler, and lead everyone in prayer. He would often stay afterward, and you could get a chance to speak to him for a few moments.

It was at one of these rosary services, in October 1994, that I was struck by a change that had come over the Holy Father, and by the toll that the previous year had taken on him. It was the only time I ever remember seeing him in poor spirits. Physically, he was struggling. The year before, in Denver, he had dragged the much younger Archbishop Stafford off hiking in the Rockies. Now, he shuffled into the room, limping after his hip surgery, favoring his bad shoulder, his left hand shaking from what people were speculating was Parkinson's disease.

Politically—and I think that's the right word to use—he'd had a tough year, too. The long fight over the Cairo conference was only one setback. He was very worried about the war-torn Balkans and had recently tried to visit the three capitals of the area—Belgrade, Sarajevo, and Zagreb—but the Orthodox Church wouldn't let him come to Belgrade, and the pope was persuaded that Sarajevo was too dangerous. Ringed by hills, the city was vulnerable to bombs being lobbed down on it by Bosnian Serbs. Even though the pope was willing to risk his own safety, he wasn't willing to jeopardize the safety of the crew of his plane, those traveling with him, and residents of the city itself. The pope did visit Zagreb, but I was told by Archbishop Vinko Puljic of Sarajevo, "His mind was so strong, but his body hurt." A few weeks after that, the Vatican announced that John Paul II would not be going to the United States that fall to address the United Nations. His health just wouldn't allow it.

That night at the rosary service, neither the pope's physical condition or political difficulties affected his ability to lead us in prayer. His voice was strong. His prayers, as always, were intense. Afterward, on his way out of the room, the Holy Father stopped to say hello to Kathy and me. I couldn't help noticing how sad his face was, how tired he seemed. "I am sorry, Mr. Ambassador," he said. "The pope is not going to America this year. The pope is too ill. The pope is old. He is too old."

I didn't know how to reply. All I could think to do was to try and cheer him up. "Maybe next year, Holy Father," I said, "when your strength returns."

"I don't know," he said, shaking his head. Then he repeated, "Too ill, too old. But I have done my best. I have done everything I could for Christ and for the church."

It was an awkward moment. I began to feel overcome at the idea of the world's strongest leader expressing such feelings of vulnerability. I started to choke up and could feel my eyes filling with tears. I knew other people were behind us, waiting for their chance for a word with the Holy Father, but I didn't want to end the conversation like that. I thought twice about whether it was appropriate to presume to give the pope encouragement, but I decided to try it. The pope had shaken my hand, and now I grabbed his hand with both of mine. "You have to go back to America, Holy Father," I said. "They love you there. Remember Denver and all the young people," I said, referring to 1993, "and all the singing. And before that, in Boston. Remember the rain. American needs you, Holy Father. You give Americans hope."

The pope forced a wan smile and nodded his head, then he moved on, shaking hands, blessing people, blessing the rosaries that they had used during the service, and then he was gone.

I wasn't the only one who noticed the drop in the pope's spirits. Tad Szulc, who was finishing up his biography of John Paul II at that time, did too. One day, he came for lunch at Villa Richardson, and he shared his thoughts with me about the Holy Father.

"Clearly, he's not the same," Szulc said. "He's disappointed about not being able to travel. Belgrade didn't want him. Sarajevo's not safe. The patriarch doesn't want to meet. He couldn't make it to the United States. But there's something else. He seems preoccupied. I think he's thinking about the end . . . when he goes. It's as if he's watching himself deteriorate, seeing how the job has used him up, taken everything out of him. There's almost this air of a martyr about him."

In a way, I was glad to hear that I wasn't the only one worried about the Holy Father's well-being, that I wasn't imagining something that wasn't there. In another way, though, that made me even more worried. I decided to call two of the people closest to the pope in the American church and two of my closest friends, Bernard Cardinal Law of Boston and John Cardinal O'Connor of New York, to express my concerns. "I could be way off base," I said to both of them, "but

I think there's something wrong. He just seems so down . . . so depressed. It's not like him."

Just as Tad Szulc had done, both cardinals mentioned the pope's health and his disappointment at not being able to travel. But I argued that it was more than that. I didn't use the word *martyr* as Tad Szulc had done; instead, I put it in more political terms. "I think he's worried about his legacy. I think—with his health the way it is—he's feeling like a lame duck, but he still wants to do more. He wants peace in the Balkans, he wants to see the church into the millennium, he wants to go to the Holy Land. . . . He's go so much on his plate—and, given the way his health has been going, he's not sure how much he'll be able to get done." "I don't know what I'm asking," I told both Law and O'Connor, "but I just wondered if there was anything that you could do."

Both cardinals listened sympathetically, but I knew there wasn't anything they could say in reply. I was their friend, but I wasn't part of the family and they never talked out of school. I knew that the official attitude of those in the church about the pope's well-being is "the pope is always in perfect health—until the day he dies," so I didn't expect them to respond. I just wanted to give them a heads-up in case they could be of any help to the Holy Father, even if it was just to try to boost his spirits.

A few weeks later, Tad Szulc told me that he had expressed the same concerns and met the same reaction from his friends inside the church. He said he couldn't get anybody to comment on the pope's health or frame of mind, either on or off the record, and that he had considered trying to describe what he felt the pope was going through in his book, but had decided against it. "People will say I'm not a psychologist," he said, "and that I'm certainly not the pope's psychologist." In the end, all he wrote in the book about the last months of 1994 was that "the year closed in a mood of political pessimism and personal suffering."

To this day, I think Tad Szulc and I were right, that John Paul II was going through a troubling period at the time. Somehow, though, the pope found the strength to pull through it—to bounce back. It wasn't a matter of his injuries healing or his somehow discovering the Fountain of Youth. It was more a matter of his accepting the circumstances he found himself in—the poor health, the difficult secular and religious politics—and then saying "It's not going to stop me, and I'm not going to feel sorry for myself." And that's just what he did. If he couldn't climb the three stairs up to the altar anymore, why, they'd just have to build him an elevator. If he couldn't walk well enough to make the rounds after an audience anymore, why, they'd just have to rig up some kind of moving platform to get him around. Monsignor Robert Tucci and the papal advance did just that.

It was as if the pope was saying: "You—Tucci—figure it out. I'm not slowing down just because my body is, not when my mind's still sharp as a tack, not while Christ is in my soul. Just get me up on the stage and the show will go on. Just get me up to Mount Sinai and I'll do the rest." Like Mohammed, if he couldn't climb the mountain, he'd make the mountain come to him. John Paul wouldn't take no for an answer at the end of 1994—and because of that, he pulled himself through a difficult time and went on to pull the church into the twenty-first century.

20

A DEDICATION AT THE ANGELICUM

"Saint Thomas was not one of my professors!"

I saw how strongly and how quickly the pope was able to bounce back a few weeks later. In November, an International Congress of the Dominican Order was held in Rome. It began with the beatification of Father Hyacinthe Marie Cormier, founder of the Dominican-run Pontifical University at St. Thomas Aquinas, the Holy Father's alma mater. A few days later, the college, popularly known as the Angelicum, dedicated the John Paul II Auditorium and the Holy Father attended the ceremony held in his name.

The campus of the Angelicum, near the *Quirinale*, is made up of a series of arched red, orange, and ochre tile-roofed buildings connected by courtyards of palm trees and gravel walks. Walking through the halls, seeing the tablets on the walls of other popes who had attended the school—Pius XII, John XXIII, and Paul VI—a person is reminded of the school's tradition. Experiencing the serenity of the place, it's difficult to imagine how different it must have been just after World War II when the young Father Wojtyla was a student there. I was told that he'd been sent to the Dominican-run Angelicum because his patron, the archbishop of Kraków, Adam Stefan Sapieha, disapproved of the other pontifical seminary in Rome, the more "liberal" Jesuit-run Gregorian.

The night of the dedication ceremony was unusually cold for Rome. Inside the Angelicum though, there was an electricity in the air as seminarians and faculty strode quickly through the hallways taking care of last-minute details and cars pulled into the cobblestone driveway to drop off invited guests. Before entering the auditorium, I was greeted by Professor Edward Kaczynski, O.P., the rector; and by the chancellor, Father Timothy Radcliffe, O.P., the head of the Dominican Order around the world. "Too bad all your graduates are poor priests," I joked with them. "If you had some rich businessmen as alumni, this would be a good night for a fund-raiser for the college."

The two priests laughed, and Father Radcliffe said, "It's still a great night for the school, even if we don't make money from it."

I took my seat in the front row of the large, semicircular hall. It had a high ceiling with tall, arched clerestory windows set high up on the walls and row upon row of curved oak benches with backs rising up from the auditorium floor. After a short wait, I could tell by the increasing number of priests streaming in through the doorways that the Holy Father was about to arrive. While we waited, I found out that this was only the pope's second time back at the school since he received his doctorate in ethics in 1948.

The pope entered from a door only a few feet from where I sat. Everyone stood and applauded, the students most of all. The Holy Father smiled broadly and waved to the packed audience. He came over and shook hands with me, then worked his way around the rest of the front row of seats, shaking hands and embracing old friends, before taking his place up on the small speaker's platform. After a brief but very warm introduction, the Holy Father stood behind the podium, looking very much like the professor he used to be and everyone in the audience stood, applauded, and cheered. The Holy Father smiled broadly. After some minutes, the cheering subsided. It was time to hear the Holy Father preach.

The pope began his address by saying that he was glad to be at the university where he studied as a young man. "Contrary to what some say, Saint Thomas was *not* one of my professors!" The crowd, especially the young seminarians, roared with laughter at the pope's joke.

In his speech, the Holy Father greeted "the members of the whole Dominican family" and told us that he was going to "retrace with you the stages of the great contribution made to evangelization by the

sons of Saint Dominic" as well as discuss the "task of the new evangelization" in the world today. He spoke about the progression of that
evangelization in Europe, Africa, and Asia, as well as on the "new
continent" of America. He mentioned the dialogue he had initiated
with Islam and with the Jews, then he paid tribute to a number of
Dominican leaders throughout history, like Fathers Lacordaire and
Cormier, and included two women, Marie Poussepin and Sister Agnes
de Jesus Galand de Langeac, praising their work in Latin America.

As he spoke, I watched him closely. He seemed to be standing
straighter, and his face seemed brighter, more alive, than it had in recent weeks. Whether he had taken the rest he needed to recover—
physically and emotionally—or whether he was drawing strength
from the young people in the audience, I couldn't tell. Whatever the
cause, he appeared to be back in stride, to have on his "game face." It
was as if he were saying, "I studied here, too, you know, and I learned
a few things—and tonight I'm going to share them with you." His
voice was strong, his gestures sharp. At one point, I looked over at
Monsignor Dziwisz and saw him nodding his head "yes, yes" after the
Holy Father made a particular point—as if Dziwisz were saying, "All
right! He's got his fast ball tonight."

The Holy Father turned his attention to the present. "The apostles
of our age face a situation which is very different from that of the
past," he said, and he explained that they must address themselves to
three different constituencies—those who do not believe, those who
no longer believe, and those who believe but cannot conform their
lives to the Gospel. He spoke about the crisis in modern culture that
embraced reason when it came to science but rejected the "moral and
transcendent dimensions" of reason. "Dominican charism," he said,
"must rediscover its vocation to study the truth, the absolute, the very
reasons of life." Then he invoked the name of one of the greatest
practitioners of reason in the church's history, St. Thomas Aquinas,
and told the seminarians his "passionate devotion to the truth [and]
anthropology and metaphysics must become your model."

When he finished speaking, though, it wasn't St. Thomas or any of
the other philosophers of the church or of the Dominican Order
whom he chose to invoke—it was the Blessed Mother. "I entrust your

efforts to Mary, Queen of Apostles," he said. "May she walk by your side and enable you to bring to contemporary man the life-giving message of the Gospel with joy and strength."

The pope's speech received a standing ovation from the members of the Angelicum community. Afterward, the Holy Father stayed to greet as many people from the audience as he could. When it came my turn to see him, the Holy Father took hold of my hand with both of his and pulled me over to where Father Radcliffe was standing. "Look what I have," he said to Father Radcliff mysteriously, "the proof, the proof."

Father Radcliffe looked at us quizzically. He didn't know what to say, didn't know what the pope was talking about.

"We were both taught by the Dominicans," the pope finally explained. "The ambassador is proof that it is not only the Jesuits who make the politicians. The Dominicans make them, too."

Everyone had a good laugh at the pope's joke. It was great night, a great homecoming for the Holy Father, who was playing on his home field in front of a hometown crowd. As I was leaving the college that night, I ran into my friend, the Reverend John Farren, O.P., a Dominican priest who now works with the Knights of Columbus in New Haven, Connecticut. "Get your tickets now for Jubilee 2000," Father Farren said. "John Paul the Great is going to be with us for a while, thanks be to God."

21

A MOTHER'S LOVE IS A BLESSING

Easing a mother's pain

I had witnessed the Holy Father's ability to lift the spirits of those who were suffering many times throughout the four and half years I spent in Rome and at the Vatican. In March 1995, I got a chance to see him do it again, close up, for a family friend.

My wife, Kathy, is part of a group of nine or ten women who have remained friends and stayed close throughout their lives. They all went to school together, from first grade through high school, taught by the Sisters of Notre Dame at St. Augustine's School in South Boston. They've been in each other's wedding parties, they remember each other's birthdays and anniversaries, and go to each other's children's christenings, birthday parties, weddings and baby showers. They call themselves "The Kids," even though they're all in their late fifties now, with families of grown children and young grandchildren, and even though some have moved away from South Boston, they all get together regularly. They don't think there's anything unusual about their beautiful, loyal friendship. It's the way they were brought up. It's the way they think things are supposed to be.

Since Kathy was in Rome, "The Kids" decided they would all come for a visit. None are financially that well off, but since they'd be staying with us instead of in a hotel, they figured they could afford it. At first, though, one of the women in the group wasn't going to come. Kathy's friend, Charlene Bizokas, who had already experienced a lot of family tragedy in her life, had recently lost her son, Ralph, in a car crash. She was deeply despondent. According to Kathy, Charlene couldn't stop thinking about her son's death. After much persuasion, Kathy and the others finally convinced Charlene to come to Rome, though. "It will do you good," they promised.

A few days after "The Kids" arrived, John Paul presided over a major event in St. Peter's Square with many important religious and secular leaders from all over the world attending. Normally, Kathy and I would sit in the front row with the other members of the diplomatic corps and their spouses, but because we wanted to be with our guests, we were given seats five or six rows back. That was fine with Kathy's girlfriends, they were thrilled to be that close to the Holy Father. I had hoped our seats would be on the aisle, so I might be able to introduce the women to the pope, as he walked by either before or after the ceremony. When we arrived at St. Peter's and I found that we were seated in the middle of the section, I figured it just wasn't meant to be.

After about an hour wait, the ceremony began and our visitors were, in fact, thrilled to see John Paul and by the pomp and pageantry. During much of the long service, the pope sat off to the side of the altar in the armchair provided for him, not very far away from where we were sitting. Monsignor Dziwisz stood next to him. As is his custom, Dziwisz stood scanning the crowd. He's very sharp that way; no matter how much is going on around him, he doesn't miss a thing. "Santa Lucia must have given you an extra pair of eyes," I joked to him once. "One pair in front and one pair in the back of your head." Well, that particular day, Monsignor Dzwisz's eyes were working overtime. And through eye contact and an exchange of nods, we somehow carried on a little nonverbal conversation.

When he first spotted me in the audience, the monsignor kind of raised an eyebrow and nodded toward the front row, as if to ask why I wasn't in my usual seat. I looked to either side and spread my arms out to signify that I was with friends. Dziwisz nodded that he understood. A few minutes later, he went behind the altar and spoke with a priest. The priest then crossed the back of the stage, and walked down the aisle toward us. I made my way out to the aisle to meet him.

"Ambassador," he said softly, "you are here with friends?"

"Yes," I said, "dear friends of my wife, all mothers from Boston."

The priest nodded—and waited, asking without coming right out and saying it, "Is there anything we can do?"

I moved closer and whispered to him. "One of the women has recently lost her son. She is very sad." In these situations, "Vatican shorthand" is used. You don't have to ask "Can she meet the pope?" or anything so direct. They know exactly what you're talking about.

The priest didn't say a word, he just nodded and went back to the *sagrato*, or stage. By this time the Mass was over, and the master of ceremonies was reading the names of the various groups from different countries that were in the audience. The Holy Father sat in his chair surveying the whole piazza. I watched as the priest went over to Dziwisz, and whispered something in his ear. Then I saw Dziwisz bend down and whisper something to the pope. The Holy Father looked in my direction and nodded. A few minutes later, the priest came back.

"Mr. Ambassador," he said, "if you and your party would be so kind. Please go and wait up on the steps by the *Porta Sancta*." The *Porta Sancta*—or "holy door"—is the right-hand door to St. Peter's Basilica. Except during Holy Years, it is sealed by a wall of bricks. The pope, himself, begins the work of opening the door, using a silver hammer to break through the first of the bricks. Passage through the door is symbolic of the passage from sin to grace.

When the ceremony was over, and while various dignitaries were lining up on the stage to be presented to the Holy Father, I told Kathy's friends to follow me. We made our way up to the steps of St. Peter's. The Swiss Guards recognized me and let us through.

The recessional began with the line of priests, bishops, cardinals, and the Holy Father making its way into the basilica. Kathy's friends were thrilled to be even this close to the pope. Imagine their surprise when, just as he reached the open middle door of St. Peter's, John Paul stopped, veered off at a ninety-degree angle, and walked toward us. "Oh, my god," one of Kathy's friends whispered loudly, "he's coming this way."

I stepped forward and greeted the Holy Father then turned and introduced him to Kathy's friends saying, "They're all good Catholic mothers from Boston."

"Ah, mothers from Boston," the Holy Father repeated after me.

"Do you like it here in Rome? You must like it. You don't have to cook when you come to Rome." We all laughed at the joke, and the pope laughed, too.

Then, turning serious, he said, "Mothers, the most important job. Never forget, it is the most important job." Kathy's friends were delighted when he said that, of course. I couldn't help thinking about the time I first heard him say that to Kathy ten years before.

I introduced each of the women then, individually. "This is Mrs. McDonnell. This is Mrs. Morelli. This is Mrs. O'Shea . . ." Each of them genuflected very respectfully and kissed the Holy Father's ring. When I introduced Mrs. Bizokas, I lowered my voice just a little. The Holy Father understood. After Charlene kissed his ring, the pope stepped closer to her. He put one hand on the side of her face. With the other he was holding his silver crozier, at the top of which was the figure of Jesus Christ dying on the cross. John Paul leaned his forehead against Charlene's. "Mothers are given much love but also much pain," he said softly, but loudly enough for the rest of us to hear: "Like Mary suffered when her son died. I know you have suffered, as Mary suffered. But like Mary, you will see your son again."

The Holy Father's face seemed to reflect the pain that was in Charlene's heart. It was as if he were absorbing it, taking it from her. Charlene was sobbing, but you could almost feel her releasing some of the pain. The idea that the Holy Father, the pope, the leader of her church around the world, would reach out to her in her grief, here, before the holy door of St. Peter's Basilica, clearly helped to make the burden she was carrying lighter.

Tears streamed down Charlene's face. Tears streamed down the faces of Kathy and all the rest of her friends and welled up in my eyes. I was moved by the Holy Father's compassion, and his knowledge of just what was needed, just what to say. But I was also amazed at his ability to change gears, to go from a public moment before fifty thousand people in St. Peter's Square to a private moment like this in a matter of seconds.

22

THIRD PAPAL VISIT TO THE UNITED STATES

The conscience of America

Americans like to be able to categorize people in simple ideological terms like "conservative" or "liberal." But trying to define John Paul II that way just doesn't work. I've always admired his uncompromising—some would say *conservative*—positions on moral issues like abortion. But I've always felt that his compassionate—some would say *liberal*—positions on issues of social and economic justice never got the attention they deserved, especially from the Western media. Politically, some *Vaticanisti* (Vatican watchers) divide John Paul II's papacy into two halves: a "conservative" first half, pre-1989, spent fighting the Godlessness of communism; and a "liberal" second half, post-1989, spent fighting what the pope once called "savage capitalism." Although that division is an extreme simplification, the pope's visit to the United States in the fall of 1995 was clearly an example of the second half.

To understand the significance of that trip, you have to remember the political context in which it occurred. Then-Speaker of the House Newt Gingrich was leading a self-proclaimed "Republican Revolution." He was the most powerful politician in America at the time, would be *Time* magazine's 1995 "Man of the Year." The notions that America was supposed to welcome "the poor huddled masses, yearning to breathe free" and that government was supposed to take care of those in need were being challenged, replaced by the new catchphrases of "personal responsibility" and the *Contract With*

America. The Democratic Party was in full retreat and President Bill Clinton was arguing in the press that he was still "relevant" to the political debate going on in the U.S. John Paul II was well aware of what was going on in America because he was hearing about it from U.S. church officials, reading about it in his daily news summaries, and being told about it by Vatican officials who made it a point to socialize with Americans, like me, and bring back their dinner table conversation to the pope.

I know for a fact that the pope heard about the uproar caused by a speech I gave in April 1995. Speaking to a group of American graduate students studying in Rome, I remarked that the political atmosphere Paul VI had encountered in America thirty years before was much different than the one John Paul II would experience in 1995, and I asked, "Have we gone from a 'War on Poverty' to a 'War on the Poor'?"

My speech caused quite a stir, and generated a lot of negative heat both from the "Catholic right" and from U.S. Senator Jesse Helms, a long-time opponent of the United States even *having* diplomatic relations with the Holy See. The powerful chairman of the Senate Foreign Relations Committee demanded that the State Department reprimand me for making "partisan remarks." The department complied and a "letter of reprimand" went into my file, something of which I'm sure the pope was aware. But I got a lot more letters of support from people ranging from Cardinal Bernadin and Mrs. Clinton to priests, nuns, and ordinary citizens. My other satisfaction from that controversy came from thinking it might have helped alert the Holy Father and his staff to the political environment the pope was going to encounter in the United States, an environment that I knew he was going to do his best to change.

The pope was to arrive in the United States at Newark International Airport on Wednesday, October 4, the Feast of St. Francis. I flew to Newark with President Clinton on *Air Force One* to meet the Holy Father, and spent most of the short flight from Washington in the president's private cabin, going over his planned welcoming remarks. The speech was fine as far as it went, but I suggested that the president include some of the Prayer of St. Francis in it. He liked the idea and immediately started writing the words in the margins of the top sheet of paper:

> *Lord make me an instrument of your peace.*
> *Where there is injury, pardon . . .*

Abruptly, the president stopped though. "What goes next?" he asked, stumped. "What's the next line?" Even though I knew the prayer by heart, I couldn't come up with it on command. It was on the tip of my tongue, but it just wouldn't come out.

Mrs. Clinton was with us, and she couldn't remember what came next, either. Then the president's chief of staff, Leon Panetta, came in, and he tried, too. We all tried to recite the prayer from the beginning, but hit the same brick wall. Finally, somebody, I think it was Leon, said: "I can't *say* it, but I can *sing* it." He started to sing, and we all joined in, and sure enough, the words came to us and the president wrote them all down. Later, back in Rome, I described what had happened to a Franciscan priest, who said: "*Air Force One* is thought of as a 'Flying White House,' a place where a great deal of power resides, including nuclear power. It sounds as if it can also be a place from which the power of prayer can be invoked."

We arrived in Newark about a half an hour before the pope's plane was scheduled to touch down, and waited with the two thousand or so political and religious leaders, teachers, and schoolchildren. It was a drab, drizzling day. When the pope's plane landed, the U.S. military band played the Vatican and American anthems. The door of the plane opened, and the Holy Father appeared in the doorway. The crowd cheered, especially the children, whose high-pitched cheers sounded more like shrieks and whistles. It all added a certain gaiety to an otherwise gray day.

The Holy Father stood in the doorway and smiled, waved and blessed the crowd, then he made his way down the steps—slowly, but without any help. President Clinton met him on the tarmac and escorted him along the receiving line, which was made up of two distinct groups—the first, federal and state elected and appointed officials; the second, the hierarchy of the American Catholic Church.

According to protocol, I should have been at the head of the line, next to the president and Mrs. Clinton, but I wanted to watch the crowd's reaction, so I gave up my place and stood at the end of the line, the last "suit" before the "red hats."

As he followed the president down the line, the Holy Father greeted everyone with a wave or a handshake. When he spotted me, though, he stepped right up and gave me a big two-cheeked Italian bear hug. Everyone stared at us and people whispered to one another in the crowd. The pope just laughed, turned to President Clinton, and explained: "We think of Ambassador Raymond as one of us."

The president started laughing, too, and so did I. It was definitely one of those "Kodak moments," and, luckily for me, a Vatican photographer captured it on film. But as with anything this pope did, it had a deeper meaning as well. John Paul II knew I had gotten into hot water for expressing my displeasure at the way America was treating its poor and its newcomers, and he was sending a message to the president, the State Department, and anybody else that he was in my corner.

The Holy Father moved on to greet the U.S. church officials, then he and President Clinton walked to the podium, which—unlike the one in Denver—had a canopy over it to provide shelter from the rain. I walked beside the pope, and at one point, he touched my arm with his hand and asked: "Are we on schedule? Will we have enough time?" I didn't know what he was worried about until he explained. "Today is *Rosh Hashanah*. We must finish so those who need to can be home before the sun goes down."

I couldn't get over the pope's thoughtfulness and the respect he showed for another religion. He had just flown for several hours after a demanding three-day visit to Mexico, had just been greeted by the president of the United States, and was about to deliver his first speech to the waiting crowd—but his primary concern was that any Jewish people involved in the event be able to get home before dark as their faith required.

John Paul II and President Clinton took their places on the low stage. The president spoke first, and joked: "You seem to bring the rain, but we need the rain, and we thank you for it." When it came time for the Holy Father to speak, he didn't waste any time getting "on message," as they say in politics. He spoke about the "profound changes" taking place in the world today, and the need to take advantage of the "opportunities for justice." But then he switched from foreign to local affairs. Without mentioning any names or referring directly to the *Contract With America*, he launched into the message that he was going to deliver at nearly every stop on this trip. "In a nation of immigrants," he declared, "it would indeed be sad if the United States were to turn away" from its traditional generosity. "It is my prayerful hope," the Holy Father proclaimed, "that America will persevere in its own best traditions of openness and opportunity." He called for a society "in which none are so poor that they have nothing to give and none are so rich that they have nothing to receive."

If I had been a member of Congress, I would have looked for the nearest hole in the ground to crawl into. I was glad I wasn't. I was also glad that I was sitting in a spot from which I could watch both John Paul II and Roger Cardinal Mahony of Los Angeles. Cardinal Mahony, the chairman of the U.S. Bishops Conference Committee on Pro-Life Activities, was the most outspoken voice for immigrants in the country. He'd gone way out front in fighting Proposition 187, the California ballot initiative to cut illegal immigrants off from not only welfare but also health care and public education for their children.

Cardinal Mahony was a hero, especially in the Hispanic community, as this story told about him at the Vatican shows. Supposedly, a young man who was interested in becoming a priest went to see the cardinal for advice. The young man spoke in English, but Mahony kept answering him in Spanish. Finally, the young man said, "Your Eminence, I'm sorry but I don't speak Spanish." To which Mahony replied, "Well, if you want to be a priest in Los Angeles, you better learn!" I didn't know if the story is true, but I did know that some people, both in Rome and in California, thought Mahony had gone too far out on the immigration issue and they were hoping the Holy Father would rein him in.

That's why, as the Holy Father was speaking, I kept my eyes on Mahony. His face was beaming, he nodded his head, forward and back, as if saying "Yes! Yes!" His boss was backing him up, and it obviously made the cardinal feel ten feet tall. But if Mahony was thinking, "It doesn't get much better than this," he was wrong—because it did. After the pope finished speaking and before the applause had even died down, the Holy Father walked right over and gave Cardinal Mahony a big hug, the same kind he had given me a few minutes earlier.

The pope made his way through the crowd and got into a black limousine for the first leg of his trip. The rest of us were shown to our cars, and the motorcade drove out of the airport. Despite the gray day, thousands of people had turned out along the streets of Newark, many of them Hispanic and holding flowers or waving yellow-and-white flags.

Our destination was Archbishop Ted McCarrick's residence, where the pope and the president would hold their private meeting. The rectory was located in a poor, run-down neighborhood. A few weeks before, I had attended a meeting at Cardinal Baum's apartment on the *Via della Conciliazione* where the itinerary had been discussed. I wish I'd been at the luncheon the next day, when the trip was discussed with the pope, to witness the Holy Father's subtle, but firm management style—but Cardinal O'Connor of New York told me all about it. It seems that at one point, Archbishop McCarrick was describing the difficult job he had running an archdiocese where most of the middle class had fled to the suburbs and left a parish composed primarily of the poor and the newly arrived. John Paul listened patiently at first, but then, "while tearing a piece of bread in his hands," according to Cardinal O'Connor, "looked up at McCarrick and playfully said: 'If things are so bad, Ted, maybe I ought to have John take over,'" and nodded toward Cardinal John Krol, the retired Archbishop of Philadelphia, the pope's good friend and one of his earliest supporters, and who was now confined to a wheelchair. Gently chided, Archbishop McCarrick yielded the floor.

Now, we were at McCarrick's residence in Newark. A brief ceremony was held and pictures were taken. Before the pope and the president went into their meeting, I had a chance to speak to the Holy Father.

"I told you last year that America needed you to come back and to hear your message, Holy Father," I said, "and now you're here—on the Feast of Saint Francis."

The pope smiled and nodded his head. "Even the pope sometimes needs encouragement," he said. "And the world needs more Saint Francises."

He and President Clinton held their meeting, which was much less charged than their previous encounters in Denver and Rome. When they came out, they released a joint statement. In it, President Clinton expressed his "admiration for the pope's tireless endeavors to improve the lives of the poor and disadvantaged, especially in developing nations." The president's words would prove to be prophetic, given the pope's message over the next few days—although, as it turned out, he could have said "in developed as well as developing nations."

The next stop was just around the block at Sacred Heart Cathedral, an impressive Gothic building with spires taller than Notre Dame in Paris. A white canopy was set up in front of the church as protection against the rain that was coming down off and on. The popemobile pulled up out front, the Holy Father emerged from the car and then made his way up the steps to the cathedral as people cheered and the organ played joyous music. Inside the church, the pope received a thunderous ovation from the two thousand people packed inside, many of them priests and nuns. It took him ten minutes just to make his way down the center aisle, he shook so many hands and blessed so many people on the way. Everyone stood on their tiptoes, leaned over, and craned their necks to get a better look at the pope. Some people cried with joy. I was sitting in the front row of the cathedral with the president and Mrs. Clinton. Just before he stepped up to the altar, the Holy Father stopped to greet us once again.

I took the opportunity to introduce the pope to Seton Hall University President Thomas Peterson, O.P. "Father Peterson was my ethics and logic teacher at Providence College," I said.

A sly smile crept across the Holy Father's face. "If Raymond was such a good student, why did you let him enter politics?" he asked Dr. Peterson.

The service was somber, with the smoke and thick smell of incense filling the air. When it came time for him to speak, the pope continued to call for an America that continued to welcome and continued to care. He called the Newark cathedral a "symbol of the living church, which is open to everyone without exception, to men and women of every race and tongue, of every people and nation," and he paid tribute to "the extraordinary human epic that is the United States of America."

"Early Americans were proud of their strong sense of individual responsibility," the pope said, "but that did not lead them to build a radically individualistic society. They built a community-based society, with a great openness and sensitivity to the needs of their neighbors." Then the pope invoked the most powerful symbol of that openness. "Close to the New Jersey shore, there rises a universally known landmark which stands as an enduring witness to the American tradition of welcoming the stranger, and which tells us something important about the kind of nation America has aspired to be. The United States is called to be a hospitable society, a welcoming culture." Finally, the pope invoked the saint's day being celebrated. "Saint Francis of Assisi, whose feast we celebrate today, shines forth as a great lover and artisan of peace," he said. "Let us invoke his intercession upon the United Nations' work for justice and peace throughout the world."

But before he finished speaking, the Holy Father turned his attention from the larger arena of world affairs to the smaller area of everyday life. He thanked the hundreds and hundreds of volunteers from parishes in New Jersey and New York who were working so hard to make his visit a success. Before leaving the church, I watched him stop to thank one particular family. They were Hispanic, a husband, wife, and daughter, and I watched the Holy Father speak with them, bless them, and bless a medal they held out to him, an image of Our Lady of Guadalupe.

The next day the Holy Father visited the United Nations; it was the eve of its fiftieth anniversary. Some people who had seen him during his visit to the U.N. sixteen years before remarked at the changes in his physical presence. But although he had passed from being a vigorous, former quarry worker turned pope into an elder statesman, he was still the moral leader of the world. The pope walked slowly to the rostrum, but once he began speaking, he took command. Standing in front of the tall blue curtain on which was displayed the U.N. symbol, his voice was strong and forceful right from the start, and he raised and lowered his voice and used gestures to emphasize his words more than he had in recent years. I wasn't surprised, though, because I'd been alerted by friends at the Vatican who worked with him on his speech that the Holy Father had put in extra rehearsal time for this one. It showed.

The Holy Father began his address to the General Assembly by describing the great changes that the world was witnessing on "the threshold of a new millennium" and how "men and women throughout the world, even when threatened by violence, have taken the risk of freedom." He linked the "values which inspired those people's liberation movements" to the commitments contained in the United Nations Charter—in "fundamental human rights . . . in the dignity and worth of the human person . . . [and] to promote social progress and better standards of life in larger freedom." The Holy Father spoke about "terrible crimes committed in the name of lethal doctrines which taught the 'inferiority' of some nations and cultures during World War II," and he deplored the fact that, "unhappily, the world has yet to learn how to live with diversity, as recent events in the Balkans and Central African have painfully reminded us."

Then, in a remarkable passage in which he showed himself to be both theologian and politician, he explained how "every culture is an effort to ponder the mystery of the world and in particular of the human person. . . . The heart of every culture is its approach to the greatest of all mysteries: the mystery of God." He proclaimed, "True patriotism never seeks to advance the well-being of one's own nation at the expense of others. For in the end this would harm one's own nation as well: doing wrong damages both aggressor and victim."

The pope condemned the "devastating political consequences" of "an aggressive nationalism." Then added, "No less grave are the results of economic utilitarianism, which drives more powerful countries to manipulate and exploit weaker ones." As he delivered these words, I noticed a change in the audience. Throughout his address everyone had been listening attentively, following along on their translated texts. But from where I sat, next to then-U.N. Ambassador Madeleine Albright, I noticed that when the Holy Father delivered these words, many of the delegates from the less developed countries leaned forward in their seats with increased interest. Some of these delegates wore clothes traditional to their countries and cultures; some wore Western suits and dresses. Some were listening to the pope's address in English, others over their headsets in translation. But all seemed particularly excited now, many of them nodding and smiling in agreement.

"For the emerging countries, the achievement of *political independence* has too frequently been accompanied by a situation of de facto *economic dependence*," the pope continued, his voice rising. "When millions of people are suffering from a poverty which means hunger, malnutrition, sickness, illiteracy, and degradation, we must remind ourselves that *no one* has a right to exploit another for his own advantage." These remarks were punctuated by loud applause from a majority of the delegates—the majority representing countries from the Third World.

The Holy Father then called upon the United Nations to "rise more and more above the cold status of an administrative institution, and to become a moral center where all the nations of the world feel at home," and to serve as the model for a "family of nations." He explained that "in an authentic family, the strong do not dominate; instead, the weaker members, because of their very weakness, are all the more welcomed and served."

"We must not be afraid of the future," the pope said in closing, echoing a theme he has used since first ascending to the throne of St. Peter. "We must not be afraid of man. It is no accident that we are here. Each and every human person has been created in the 'image and likeness' of the One who is the origin of all that is. We have within us the capacities for wisdom and virtue. With these gifts, and with the help of God's grace, we can build in the next century and the next millennium a civilization worthy of the human person, a true culture of freedom. We can and must do so! And in doing so, we shall see that the tears of this century have prepared the ground for a new springtime of the human spirit."

When the pope finished his speech, he received the usual thunderous ovation. But this audience wasn't made up of young people in Denver, or pilgrims to Rome or peasants from a poor Catholic country. This audience was made up of delegates from all of the world's governments, many of them non-Catholic. Still, the pope brought them out of their seats.

A reception followed the Holy Father's address. Delegates crowded around the pope, who was smiling, shaking hands, obviously pleased with the warm welcome he was receiving. I noticed some of the delegates were even taking out pens and pieces of paper and asking him for his autograph. One unrolled the headdress he was wearing and asked the pope to sign that! I was standing with New York's John Cardinal O'Connor and Archbishop John Foley, president of the Pontifical Commission for Social Communications, when one of the delegates approached us. "Your pope is the only one who fights for us," the delegate declared. "He knows what it is like in our countries. He has come to see us. And he makes the rich countries understand our situation."

Archbishop Foley and I shared a cab back to the hotel and were discussing the pope's speech and the great reception he got. But we were interrupted by our cabdriver, who told us he was Pakistani—and a Muslim. "You know the pope!" he exclaimed. "The pope is a good man. He is everybody's pope!"

Archbishop Foley and I just looked at each other. From U.N. delegates to cabdrivers—John Paul II was taking New York by storm.

That evening, the pope went back across the Hudson to New Jersey to speak at Giants Stadium. I stayed in New York City, in the studio of New York Cable One, to serve as a kind of "color commentator" for the live broadcast of the event and to take part in a two-hour commentary afterward. But because I was able to see the shots from all the cameras that the station had in the Meadowlands, I felt like I was there. It had rained hard all day, but—just as in Boston in 1979, just as in Denver in 1993, just as happened everywhere the pope went—the crowd didn't seem to care. More than eighty thousand people had come out to see him. Some had arrived at the stadium the first thing in the morning and had camped out in the stands, waiting all day. These weren't the high school and college kids who had come to Denver, though. They were sophisticated, supposedly even jaded New Yorkers and New Jerseyites. Looking at the crowd on the monitors in the studio, I thought of Frank Sinatra singing *New York, New York* and the line "If you can make it here, you can make it anywhere." Based on the reaction from the crowd, John Paul II obviously was "making it" in New York.

Giant video screens in the scoreboards showed the pope's motorcade pull up to the stadium. A few minutes later, there he was, standing in the glass-walled popemobile as it pulled slowly onto the field. The crowd cheered deliriously. The popemobile circled the field with the pope in back, waving and blessing the crowd. It was like the "victory lap" an athlete sometimes takes around a stadium after being given a "day." People were clapping, stamping their feet, waving banners, singing, and crying. The "John Paul II! We love you!" chant began. As soon as people sat down in their seats, they got back up, and did "the wave." Flashes from cameras made the whole stadium look like a giant laser light show. Some journalists would describe the place as an "outdoor church"—although I hadn't been in too many churches that allowed big advertising signs for cigarettes, beer, and luxury cars on their walls. It was clear, however, that it was the preacher and not the structure that made the place holy.

Finally, the popemobile pulled up to the huge altar, set up in one of the football field's end zones. It was decorated with thousands of gold and white flowers and sheltered from the rain by a triangular-shaped canopy meant to symbolize faith, hope and charity. The pope made his way up the steps and sat down on a beautiful red-and-gold throne-style chair that had been made, one of the on-location reporters told us, by a New Jersey woodworker.

The service reflected the diversity of America, with choirs singing in English, Spanish, and Polish. When it came time to deliver his homily, the pope went right back to work and didn't pull any punches. He challenged the crowd in what would be called the most "strongly worded" sermon of his trip.

"Is present-day America becoming less sensitive, less caring toward the poor, the weak, the stranger, the needy?" he wanted to know before answering emphatically—"It must not!" He went on to say, "Today, as before, the United States is called to be a hospitable society, a welcoming culture. If America were to turn in on itself, would this not be the beginning of the end of what constitutes the very essence of the American experience?"

Watching on the monitors, it seemed to me that the Holy Father looked tired, as if the trip and the big day at the U.N. had taken something out of him. As usual, though, he got stronger as he went on, as if he drew strength and energy from the positive reaction of the crowd.

As he continued, he added another group to the list of those in danger of being unwelcome in the United States. "Sadly," he said, "today a new class of people is being excluded. When the unborn child—the stranger in the womb—is declared to be beyond the protection of society not only are America's deepest traditions radically undermined and endangered, but a moral blight is brought upon society."

After the Mass, the pope helicoptered back to New York and the residence of the papal nunzio to the U.N. But the television show I was participating in continued and included a discussion among panelists Peter Steinfels, the religion reporter for the *New York Times;* his wife, Peggy, editor of *Commonweal* magazine; Bill van der Hover, curator of the FDR Library and me. The show went on for several hours and was one of the most substantive discussions about politics and religion that I'd ever participated in. It turned out that I wasn't the only one who felt that way.

The next morning, before going out to Queens for the pope's next outdoor Mass, I spoke to Archbishop Renato Martino, the Vatican's representative to the United Nations, a man who is an outstanding diplomat professionally and is personally always generous with his time. "We all liked what you had to say on television last night," Archbishop Martino told me, "including the Holy Father." I didn't ask Martino if he was serious, if the pope had actually watched some of the television coverage the previous night or if he was just pulling my leg in a good-natured joke. But a little later I ran into Cardinal O'Connor and asked him if it was true.

"Oh, it's true. I heard it, too," O'Connor said. "And it shouldn't be a surprise. You know how he is. He's always asking questions. He's always trying to find out what's going on all over the world. He wants to know *everything*. Why wouldn't he want to know if his message is getting across? Why wouldn't he watch the television coverage if he had the chance?"

After Cardinal O'Connor walked away, the image that came to my mind was of an actor hanging around until the first edition of the next day's newspaper came out, waiting to see his reviews. Some people, I guess, would like to think the pope would be above that kind of thing. But it's ridiculous to think that he wouldn't be interested in seeing how he and his message were being presented to the world. The fact that he *was* an actor, that he understands the importance of a good delivery to go along with a good message, doesn't make that message any less sincere. It just shows how hard John Paul II works at trying to serve God—and that Ronald Reagan isn't the only modern leader who could be called "the great communicator."

That morning, the pope preached to seventy-five thousand people at Aqueduct Racetrack in Queens, one of the most densely populated Catholic dioceses in the country—and one of the most diverse. As part of the Mass, six different people delivered special prayers in English, Spanish, Creole, Polish, Italian, and Korean, and the pope himself switched back and forth between English and Spanish in his remarks. A multicolored cross was hung above the altar to symbolize the diversity of the parish, and the pope sat on a huge altar built between two artificial lakes.

Instead of the rain and cold of the previous days, the pope had to contend with a glaring sun and a wind that was so strong it ruffled his vestments and forced him to take off his skullcap. But the weather didn't faze the Holy Father in the least—in fact, he referred to the weather in his homily. "Yesterday evening, very strong rain," the pope told the crowd. "Today, very strong wind." Water, he told the crowd, was a symbol of life. Wind, he said, is "a symbol of the Holy Spirit."

Once again, the pope drummed the theme of his trip home to those who had come to hear it. "For more than two hundred years," he said, "people of different nations, languages, and cultures have come here, bringing memories and traditions of the old country, while at the same time becoming part of a new nation. America has a reputation the world over, a reputation of power, prestige and wealth, richness. But not everyone here is powerful; not everyone here is rich. In fact, America's sometimes extravagant affluence often conceals much hardship and poverty."

The next day's morning Mass—before 125,000 on the Great Lawn of Central Park—was both the largest and the most picturesque event of the trip. It was rainy again, and the mist rose off the green and gold trees of the park, surrounded by the skyline of midtown Manhattan. As usual, people had arrived hours earlier, some came before dawn. They were camped out on the grass, sitting on tarpaulins or plastic sheets, wearing raincoats and ponchos, all waiting for the pope to arrive. The city of New York thoughtfully provided a few "warm-up acts." Roberta Flack, Natalie Cole, and the Boys Choir of Harlem performed. But it was clear from the ovation he got when he arrived who the real star of the show was—John Paul II. The New York crowd "went wild," as the sports announcers like to say, waving banners, screaming, and cheering as the popemobile arrived and made a circuit around the field. As usual every ethnic group was represented, holding flags from their native countries, waving yellow-and-white papal flags. This pope clearly belonged to everyone.

The Holy Father, dressed in his gold-trimmed vestments, ascended to the altar that had been set up on the south end of the lawn. "Good morning!" he said to the crowd when he was seated on the stage. "Good morning!" the crowd good-naturedly roared back. "No rain, no sun," the pope said, waving to the sky. Then, with the timing of a nightclub comedian: "Thanks be to God." The crowd roared again, and launched into the now familiar chant: "John Paul Two! We love you!"

In Central Park, the pope directed his message to young people. Recalling his trip two years before to Denver, he reminded everyone that "many people wondered and worried that the young people of America would not come to the World Youth Day, or, if they did come, that they would be a problem. Instead, the young people's joy, their hunger for the truth, their desire to be united all together in the Body of Christ, made clear to everyone that many, very many young people of America have values and ideals which seldom make the headlines."

"I know this is not *Denver*," he said, lowering his voice theatrically, pretending to put down the rival city. "This is *New York!*" he said, his voice rising in praise, playing to the partisan crowd. "The *great New York!*" he said, upping the ante. "This is *Central Park* . . ." he said even more emphatically. The pope was doing what rock stars do when they say how great it is to be playing tonight in . . . whatever city they're in. And the crowd loved it.

The Holy Father did something then that I'd never seen him do before: he spoke in a very personal way about himself as a young man. He referred to a song that he and his friends used to sing, a Polish version of "Silent Night." And then he actually began to sing it, in Polish, in a voice the *New York Times* would describe as a "trembling baritone."

> *In the silence of the night, a voice is heard:*
> *Get up, shepherds, God is born for you!*
> *Hurry to Bethlehem to meet the Lord!*

While he sang, the whole park was completely quiet. It felt like all of Manhattan had stopped to listen to John Paul sing. After he finished, the crowd roared—and the pope couldn't resist a joke. Waiting until it was quiet again, he ad-libbed: "And to think, you don't even know Polish."

After giving so much in the way of moral instruction to the crowd, the pope asked for something in return. He asked everyone to stand up "for marriage and family life! Stand up for purity! Resist the pressures and temptations of a world that too often tries to ignore a most fundamental truth: that every life is a gift from God our Creator, and that we must give an account to God of how we use it either for good or evil."

Speaking faster, getting into the rhythm and repetition of a preacher, the pope kept up the pressure: 'The pope asks you to do this. He knows that you will do this, and for this he loves you. Then you can tell the whole world that you gave the pope his Christmas present in

October, in New York, in Central Park." Once again, the whole center of Manhattan Island erupted.

That afternoon, the pope said the rosary with John Cardinal O'Connor and three thousand invited guests at St. Patrick's Cathedral. I was sitting way up front in the church and I couldn't help but remember how my friend Cardinal O'Connor used to say he "always expected the police to arrive and evict him as an impostor" when he was up at the altar of St. Patrick's. I wondered if being up there with the Vicar of Christ eased that anxiety.

Over the last few days, New York City had fallen for the pope in a big way. Everywhere I looked, I saw his picture. Banners and signs welcomed him. Barnes and Noble took all their other books out of their windows and displayed just one, the new biography *Pope John Paul II* by Tad Szulc—and according to the salespeople I talked to, the books were selling like hotcakes. After the rosary service, John Paul II took matters in his own hands in order to thank New Yorkers personally for their warm welcome.

Although I had been sitting up front in St. Patrick's, as soon as the service was over Ray Teatum, the assistant clerk of New York City, and I hustled out the side door and around to the front of the cathedral so we could watch the pope come out. About twenty thousand other people were there, too, backed up along the sidewalks behind the wooden police barricades as far as you could see. Since I had my Vatican pass and Ray knew the head of security for the archdiocese, a retired New York City cop, we got a great spot up on the steps of St. Patrick's. Standing right next to us was a Secret Service agent assigned to the event. Soon the pope, accompanied by Cardinal O'Connor, came out of the cathedral. Of course, a great roar went up from the crowd. But the roar grew even louder when the Holy Father, after descending the steps to the sidewalk, decided against getting into the popemobile for the short ride around the block to Cardinal O'Connor's residence for his next event and chose to walk instead.

"Oh, no!" said the Secret Service agent standing next to us. "What's he doing! He can't do that! Doesn't he know he can't do that!"

Ray and I looked at each other. Ray rolled his eyes and said to the agent, in a perfect New York accent: "He's the pope, buddy. He can do anything he damn well pleases—especially in this town, the way it's gone nuts for him."

When the crowd, which was reinforced by shoppers, tourists, and worshippers on their way to a synagogue just up Fifth Avenue, saw the pope coming out to meet them, they surged forward to try to touch him. After getting over their initial shock, the police and the security people recovered and rushed forward, forming a protective ring around the Holy Father—loose enough to allow the kind of contact with people that the pope obviously wanted, but tight enough to jump in if anything got out of hand. So off they went, the pope and Cardinal O'Connor, first south on Fifth Avenue and then east on Forty-ninth Street, with the pope reaching out to the crowds lined up along the police barriers. The pope was smiling, waving, and shaking hands. Inside the closed-in atmosphere of St. Patrick's he had seemed a little tired. But now, out on the street, surrounded by adoring New Yorkers, his batteries were recharged.

On Sunday, the last day of his trip, the pope flew to Baltimore. In one way, it was a good thing that he didn't have much time left in the United States, because the excitement he was generating sparked more and more people to try to see if they could add "just one more event" or "one more meeting" to his already overbooked schedule. Before I left New York, I received a call from someone in U.S. House Speaker Newt Gingrich's office. I don't remember the guy's name, but he had a very strong Southern accent and wanted to know if I could arrange for Speaker Gingrich and Senate Majority Leader Bob Dole to meet with the pope. I knew what that meant—John Paul and his message were getting such a good reception that the Republicans and their *Contract With America* were feeling the heat. I told the guy I would pass his request on to the right people on the pope's staff. And I did. But the schedule was already too full and the meeting could not be arranged.

A crowd of fifty thousand people came out early on Sunday morning to Camden Yards in Baltimore for the last papal Mass of the trip. Just as at Giants Stadium, they waited eagerly, watching the giant scoreboard for updates on the pope's progress getting to the field. "He is coming!" the scoreboard read when the pope's plane was approaching Baltimore. "He is here!" it said when the plane landed. When the popemobile finally peeked around the corner of the right field gate, the crowd cheered, people waved banners, marching bands played, and spectators waved gold-and-white pompoms. Early on, the event felt more like a ball game, a World Series game, than a Mass. The altar was set up in center field. Two hundred American bishops spilled out onto the field from the home team dugout. I heard one old-timer who worked at the park tell another: "I seen Ruth play. I seen Ripken break Gehrig's record. But this tops 'em all."

As usual, people seemed to hang on every word once the Holy Father began his homily. But, just to make sure, he used the words of Abraham Lincoln to drive his message home. "One hundred thirty years ago, President Abraham Lincoln asked whether a nation 'conceived in liberty and dedicated to the proposition that all men are created equal' could 'long endure,'" the pope said. "President Lincoln's question is no less a question for the present generation of Americans. Democracy cannot be sustained without a shared commitment to certain moral truths about the human person and human community. The basic question before a democratic society is: 'How ought we live together?'" Summing up, the pope explained, "Every generation of Americans needs to know that freedom consists not in doing what we like but in having the right to do what we ought."

From the ballpark, the pope went to *Our Daily Bread*, an archdiocesan soup kitchen to have lunch with William Cardinal Keeler and a group of families that included those with adopted and mentally retarded children. After various meetings, he headed for Baltimore Airport and, after a brief meeting with Vice President Gore, the return trip to Rome.

A lot of people think the pope has his own plane, *Shepherd I*, just like the president has his own plane, *Air Force One*. In reality, the pope flies commercial. When he flies from Rome, the Holy Father uses an *Alitalia* jet. When he flies from other countries, he uses one of the host country's commercial planes. The aircraft are all adapted, however, for the pope's use, with the seats of the first-class section removed and a special papal "cabin" installed.

After that 1995 trip, I flew back to Rome in the Holy Father's plane. Once we got on the plane I assumed the Holy Father would go to his cabin to rest. Instead, he patiently sat for pictures with the captain and the crew. After everyone working on the aircraft had a chance to meet him the pope retired to his cabin.

On the flight, I sat in the first row of the middle section of the plane with only a red curtain separating this section from the pope's "apartment." Through the cracks in the curtain, I caught glimpses of the Holy Father moving about, changing from his vestments, sitting down, and having dinner. I could hear him and Monsignor Dziwisz talking in Polish. The pope's doctor sat next to me, and about a half hour into the flight, Monsignor Dziwisz came out and asked the doctor to come forward into the cabin. A few minutes later, the doctor came back out and sat down next to me again. "He's fine. Fine," the doctor told me. "Tired, as you would expect. But pleased. And when Papa is in a good mood, we are all in a good mood, no?" He laughed.

Through the gap in the curtain, I saw Monsignor Dziwisz getting papers and pens for the pope and putting them on top of the writing desk, then I saw the pope come over and sit down and start writing. After about fifteen or twenty minutes, Monsignor Dziwisz came out again, this time to summon me. I got out of my seat and followed him into the cabin. The Holy Father motioned for me to sit in the chair beside him. He looked tired but pleased. "I want to thank you, Ambassador, for your help, and thank President Clinton for welcoming me, and Vice President Gore for coming to say good-bye." The pope had all these sentiments scribbled down and was reading from his notes. "And most of all the American people—in New Jersey, New York, and Maryland." He paused for a second, looking down at his notes and then up at me. "Maryland," he said. "It is Mary's land, no?"

The pope seemed to be waiting for me to speak. I had learned, by then, that even though the Holy Father didn't always come right out and ask you for your opinion, that was often exactly what he wanted to hear. I had a hunch that this was one of those times, so I decided to give him mine. "Holy Father," I began, "I've been in politics many years . . ."

The pope smiled, lifted his hand to interrupt me, and playfully said, "And good years, good years. The people must have liked you."

"Oh, I hope they did," I said. "But not nearly as much as they liked you on this trip to America. I have to tell you, Holy Father. I have been worried about my country, about the direction it has been going in, about people becoming more selfish, about government becoming less caring . . ." The pope nodded, and moved his face closer to mine, as if to better hear what I was saying. "But this visit . . . what you said . . . it was so important, so appropriate, so . . . necessary. Your message of concern and respect for the poor and needy, for immigrants . . . it has been missing recently. But people needed to hear it. You could tell by their reaction. Our country thanks *you* for coming."

The Holy Father didn't say anything at first. I knew there was no way he would say anything to imply he accepted any credit. He just leaned toward me, his piercing eyes only a few inches from mine. Finally, with a little sigh, he sat back. "Tell them I pray for them. I pray for America the beautiful."

The Holy Father didn't say anything else. After a minute or two, Monsignor Dziwisz came over. "Maybe the Holy Father wants to get some rest," Dziwisz said. The pope didn't protest, which meant it was time for me to go. But as I started to get up, the pope reached out and took my hand in both of his. "Thank you," he said. "Thank you for what you do for your country and for your church." I kissed his ring and went back to my seat.

Monsignor Dziwisz had said "Maybe the Holy Father wants to get some rest." But he didn't rest, at least not right away. For a long time, he sat at the desk writing. In my section, the plane was filled with papal staff, as well as American bishops, monsignors, and priests assigned to Rome who had been allowed to come over for the trip. They were in a jubilant mood, laughing and talking. Dinner was served, which most of them took with at least one glass of wine. Afterward, the reading lights in the plane were shut off one-by-one as people went to sleep, including the pope's doctor, who snored away in the seat next to me. The pope didn't go to sleep, though; he was still up, still writing at the desk. A young Polish priest kept going back and forth, into the pope's cabin and then to the back of the plane, taking handwritten sheets of paper from the cabin to type into a computer, then printing out sheets of paper, and bringing them up front again.

This went on for another hour or so. Then finally, John Paul got up from the desk and sat in one of the more comfortable chairs. I assumed he must be reading or praying. Finally he got up from the chair and crossed to the other side of the cabin, and out of sight. After a few minutes, I heard him get into bed and saw the lights go out.

A FRIEND IN NEED

Reaching out to my family and me

Beyond a doubt, the very best result of my job as U.S. Ambassador to the Vatican was that my whole family, my wife Kathy and all of our six children, got to know the Holy Father—and he got to know us. I was told by more than one person that the pope loved the image we projected, attending events and services together. Once, I overheard the Holy Father describe me as "the American ambassador with all the children." I knew he meant it as a compliment.

The first time the entire Flynn family was together in Rome was at Christmas 1994, and our two sons, Ray Jr. and Eddie joined Kathy, the girls and me. I asked if we could get a picture taken with the Holy Father to commemorate the event, and the pope was only too glad to oblige. After a regular Wednesday audience at Paul VI Hall, we were brought into a reception room behind the stage. When the Holy Father came in, he was beaming. He held his arms out and came over to us. "The whole family together," he said. "The way it should be."

I introduced him to my son Eddie, who was working in the U.S. Labor Department in Washington and hadn't met the pope until then, and the photographer came over and started to arrange us in a line. While we were getting into the right spots, the Holy Father had some advice for all of us. "Parents take care of children," he said. Kathy and I nodded. "Children take care of parents." And all my kids nodded politely. "Brothers take care of sisters," the pope continued. My daughters smiled while my two sons looked a little worried. "And women take care of the men." Now it was my turn and my sons' turn to laugh and my wife's and daughters' turn to look surprised—but we were all happy to have the pope teasing us this way.

In the summer of 1993, just as I was ready to leave for Rome to begin my job as ambassador to the Vatican, my oldest son, Ray, began having a really hard time. Even though he had only a year to go before he'd graduate from college, he started skipping his classes, drinking heavily, and staying out all night. Kathy and I were completely taken by surprise. Ray had never given us any real trouble before, and we didn't know what to make of this sudden change in his behavior. At first, we thought the drinking was the *cause* of all his problems and we fought with him over that. It turned out that the drinking was a *symptom,* though. He was suffering from clinical depression brought on by a chemical imbalance in his brain. But this was something we wouldn't find out until a long time passed and a lot of pain had been endured.

We tried everything we could think of to help Ray. For starters, we tried to get him to come to Rome with us. We thought the change would be good for him, that it would snap him out of whatever was bothering him. But he didn't want to leave his friends or Boston, and we couldn't make him. He wasn't a kid anymore. Kathy, the girls, and I went to Rome, Eddie went off to college in Rhode Island, and Ray was on his own in Boston.

Things would be fine for a while, and then Ray would fall apart and start acting out. We tried to get him into counseling or some kind of therapy, but he wouldn't go. Finally it reached the point where we had to have him arrested so we could get him into treatment. It was a rough time for Ray, and for all of us—and it was made rougher by the Boston media, which wouldn't let us suffer through it privately—a penalty, I know, that many public families often have to pay.

Some good came out of this nightmare, though. It brought us closer to God and made us stronger as a family. It also showed us who our real friends were—in Boston and in Rome. My brother Dennis, back in South Boston, treated Ray like his own son. Cardinal Law was incredible, he helped find us the right doctors and helped Ray get into hospitals that could treat him. Cardinal Law would visit Ray in the hospital, and bring pizza and stay around to talk sports and politics. Most important, he prayed with Ray and told him that God still loved him. Cardinal O'Connor of New York was a big help. William Cardinal Baum, the former archbishop of Washington who was now at the Vatican, referred us to Sister Yvonne Mary, a wonderful nun who did counseling work and made time to see Ray whenever he came to visit us in Rome. And then there was John Paul II.

I don't know how the Holy Father found out about Ray's difficulties. I wasn't aware that he *did* know until one day after a diplomatic corps event in the ornate *Sala Regia*. We were all lined up, in tuxedos or the traditional formal dress of our respective countries, and the pope came along it, greeting us individually. Frequently on these occasions, the pope would joke with us. If an ambassador was wearing all his decorations—the "fruit salad," as it's called in the military—the pope would say something like, "Ambassador So-and-so needs to get a bigger coat to carry all his ribbons. Maybe Cardinal Sodano will lend him one of his." Or if we were all having a formal lunch afterward, he would wish us *"Bon appetito"*—and remind us not to drink too much wine.

On this particular day, I saw him joking with the ambassadors up ahead of me in line, but when he reached me the Holy Father became serious. "Ambassador Raymond," he said, greeting me, "how is your son? I pray for him." The pope's remark caught me off guard. All I could say was, "He's . . . he's doing better, Holy Father. Thank you for asking." But to myself I thought: "What a guy! With all the problems he has to think about, he makes time to think about mine."

Not long after that, we persuaded Ray to come to stay with us in Rome for a while. He seemed better. He wasn't drinking, thank God, but he had no energy. His confidence and self-image were shot. He just didn't believe in himself anymore. After a lot of agonizing, we finally decided the best thing to do would be to get him back into a hospital in the United States. Just before Ray was going to leave Rome, the pope approached me after Mass one day at St. Peter's.

"Your son is going back to the United States?" the pope asked.

Once again, I was amazed at how much he knew about everything that was going on around him. "Yes, Holy Father," I replied, "he's going into a hospital for a while."

"He is getting good medical care?" the pope asked.

"Oh, yes," I answered. "Cardinal Law has been very helpful. He's found the best doctors in the world for us."

"But the doctors . . . the hospitals . . ." the pope said. "Much bills? Very expensive?" I didn't know where the Holy Father was going with this. I was moved that he cared enough to ask, but he had so many questions.

"Yes, Holy Father," I said, "but we'll manage, we'll manage." I stumbled, trying to find the right words to say. But what the pope said next caused me to stumble for words even more.

"Maybe the pope can help. The pope has some small money. Not church money, but the pope's small money. Maybe he can help."

Now I *really* didn't know what to say. At first I wasn't sure I had heard the pope correctly. When I realized I had heard him right, I was stunned, both by his generosity and his complete understanding of what my family was going through. He knew that we weren't wealthy, that I wasn't the typical high-roller businessman who gets appointed ambassador as a reward for raising campaign contributions, and that although I got paid a good salary, I had to pay for a house in Boston, college tuition for six kids, and now these medical bills of Ray's. I wondered if he knew that Kathy had started to work part-time in Rome.

I thanked the Holy Father, but said, "No, no. We'll be all right. We'll get by. But thank you . . . thank you so much, Holy Father." Then I took his hand and kissed his ring.

John Paul wasn't content to leave it at that, though. "If you need something," he continued, "tell Cardinal Law or Monsignor Jim [Monsignor James Harvey, a top aide to the pope and a close friend of our family]. They will let me know. But tell your son I pray for him." Then the pope blessed me and moved on.

Until now, I've told this story only to members of my family and a few close friends. I thought long and hard before revealing it here. I don't want it to be misconstrued or distorted. I don't want it to come out sounding like the pope was offering to slip some fat cat ambassador money from the collection plate while people are starving, dying from disease, and living in poverty around the world. If people read it that way, they are making a mistake. The only reason I am revealing his offer of help is because of what it reveals about Karol Wojtyla, not the pope, not even the priest, but the man.

Today, my son Ray is doing much better. He's working, taking classes to finish his college degree, and feeling much better about himself. The doctors and nurses who gave him such good medical care, and all the people who were so kind to him and to our whole family, deserve a lot of credit. Ray deserves a lot of credit, too. He might have lost confidence in himself, but he never lost his faith in God. But I believe with all my heart that the pope's prayers played the biggest part in helping my son pull through.

John Paul II didn't confine himself just to helping the Flynn family with our problems, though. He shared, and contributed to, our joy and laughter.

There was, for example, the time when Kathy was getting ready to go back to Boston for a while to be with Ray. As usual, the pope found out, and this time he decided to have some fun with his intelligence information. One day Kathy and I were at an event in St. Peter's Square and afterward the Holy Father spotted us and walked over to where we were standing. He had a kind of quizzical expression on his face, and his lips were moving, as if he were saying something, over and over again. When he got close to us we finally made it out: "Mother going home to Boston? Mother going to Boston?"

Kathy realized he was talking about her, so she answered, "Yes, Holy Father. But just for a little while. Don't worry, I'm coming back."

"But daughters staying?" the pope asked. "Daughters staying?"

"Yes, Holy Father," Kathy told him. "They're all in school and they love it here."

That's when the Holy Father hit us with the punch line. "But much boys, many boys in Rome. Daughters without their mother to watch them? Not so good. But the pope can see all of Rome from his window. Tell your daughters the pope will be watching . . . until you come back."

Well, we got the biggest kick out of his joke—but the thing is, so did he. He was still laughing when he walked away from us, toward the car that was waiting to take him back to the Apostolic Palace.

Just as the Holy Father got to know the Flynn family, we all got to know him, too. A couple of times every summer, the pope would host concerts at Castel Gandolfo, his summer residence. A canopy would be strung up over part of the courtyard to shelter the performers and the Holy Father from the sun or rain, and folding chairs would be set up for a couple of hundred people. The events were fairly casual. Many of those who attended were people from the town and priests and nuns who were studying in the area or there on retreat during the summer.

Our daughter Maureen came with Kathy and me to one of the concerts. It was a good thing, too, because afterward the Holy Father got up and made a short speech in Italian, which Maureen translated for us. Looking rested and relaxed, the pope first thanked the members of the string quartet who had played for us. Then the Holy Father talked about the importance of music. "We must have music. It is good for our souls. It reminds us of the beauty of God's world," the Holy Father said. "And through music, through making music or listening to it, we can thank God. Music is one of the best ways to pray. When you sing and when you play, you pray twice."

After the Holy Father finished speaking, and after the small crowd showered him and the quartet with applause, we got a chance to have a word with him.

"I liked what you had to say about music, Holy Father," I told him.

The pope nodded and smiled. "A priest must sing much in church," he said, "even when he cannot sing well."

"Were you a good singer, Holy Father?" I asked.

With the timing of a nightclub comic, the pope paused, then said, "When *I* sang, it was more like I was praying only *once*."

We attended another of the Castel Gandolfo concerts in the summer of 1996, this time with our daughter Katie. After that concert, the pope rose from his chair and again thanked the performers. This time, he had a special word about the value of vacations, especially for the nuns in the audience. Katie did the translating for us.

"Isn't this wonderful?" he said, gesturing with his hands around him. "The mountains, the fresh air, the lake below. We must not forget to look at nature. We must not forget to thank God for it. And we must not forget to enjoy it—and enjoy our vacation. Relax; the pope commands it. Sisters especially must relax—because we all know nuns work harder. Nuns work the hardest." Everyone in the crowd applauded then, the nuns most of all.

The last time we went up to Castel Gandolfo in the summer was on a weekday afternoon. My daughter Julie and her then-fiancé, Jamie Long, were in Rome, and I contacted my old friend Monsignor—now Bishop—Monduzzi to see if he could arrange for them to meet with the Holy Father before their wedding. "Just when we think we have gotten your whole family to see the pope, you make your family bigger," the monsignor joked. But he was able to arrange it for us.

After an outdoor Mass on a beautiful spot overlooking Lake Albano, we waited off to the side until the pope had changed from his vestments and returned to greet people. When he saw us, he came over to where we were standing, a big smile on his face and his arms outstretched to greet Kathy first, then me, then Julie, and finally Jamie.

"You are joining a good family," he said to Jamie. "God bless you and your bride and may He bring His love and happiness to you."

While we posed with him for a photo, I told the pope that Jamie was a chef at Harvard University, a place John Paul had visited when he was still Archbishop of Kraków. The Holy Father nodded, then a smile crept across his face.

"You must be a good cook," he said to Jamie. "Such a good university must have good food."

We all laughed at his joke, and Kathy and I thanked him for making time to meet Julie and Jamie.

"No, thank *you*," the Holy Father said, "for having such a wonderful family."

24

DEDICATION OF A NEW CHURCH

Always at work, always reaching out

In March 1996, a very unusual event took place in Rome—the opening of a brand-new church. Every religious order has a church of its own in Rome, and this was to be the Roman church of the *Opus Dei* (God's Work) movement. *Opus Dei* is an organization that is often misunderstood both within and outside the Catholic Church. An international society founded in 1928 in Spain, it is composed primarily of lay people who are very dedicated, devout and disciplined Catholics. Many of the members are successful professional people. *Opus Dei* and its members are not concerned with generating publicity for the good work they do, which must explain why they are sometimes labeled a "secret society." John Paul II has been a strong supporter of *Opus Dei*—and has been supported by the organization since he was Archbishop of Kraków. Once he became pope, he made the organization a "personal prelature" of the church, meaning it is a world-wide diocese, reporting directly to Rome.

The organization's new church, Blessed Josemaria Escriva, was named for the founder of the *Opus Dei* movement, who died in 1945 and was beatified by John Paul II in 1992. The church is located in Tintorito, an area on the outskirts of the city made up of new high-rise office and apartment buildings. The church building, though, was modern, made of brick, and included touches like a bell tower and arches that echoed the style of the ancient churches in Rome.

The dedication took place on a beautiful Sunday morning. The overflow crowd in attendance spilled out of the church and onto the brick plaza in the front. Monitors and loudspeakers were set up outside so even those who couldn't squeeze into the church could witness the ceremony. I had been invited to the event because I was friendly with a number of *Opus Dei* leaders and members. It wasn't until Kathy and I entered the bright, airy, high-ceilinged church that we learned that the Holy Father was coming, too.

After the usual excitement preceding his arrival, John Paul entered the church, accompanied by Camillo Cardinal Ruini, the Vicar General of Rome, and Father Alberto Ortolani, the pastor of the new parish. The Holy Father said Mass, and in his homily described the church as one "that you have been waiting for since the day your parish was established." Referring to the surrounding neighborhood, the pope talked about what a "special place" the church could become "since the area lacks the most essential services and structures for encouraging meeting and dialogue among the residents."

The Holy Father also went on to explain the day's Gospel story, in which a Samaritan woman is surprised that Jesus, a Jew, would even speak to her, because relations between the two groups were not good. Quoting Blessed Josemaria Escriva, the pope said: "'God awaits us every day. Be sure of this: There is something holy, divine, hidden in the most ordinary situations, something that each one of us must discover. There is no other way, my children; either we know how to find the Lord in our ordinary lives, or we will never find Him."

After the Mass, the Holy Father presided over the dedication ceremony, pouring chrism on the altar. When the service was over, the usual receiving line formed. As Kathy and I approached the Holy Father, he smiled and asked: "Aren't there enough old churches in Rome for you? Do you have to come to the new ones, also?"

After greeting people inside the church, the Holy Father went outside, into the courtyard in front, to greet those in the overflow crowd. He was obviously enjoying this part of his job as Bishop of Rome. He was smiling, laughing, and taking his time, greeting people and talking to them. Just as inside the church, the people outside lined up to receive his blessing. Watching from just off to the side, I saw that it was a pretty upscale crowd. *Opus Dei* is known for attracting very accomplished professional people to its ranks—doctors, lawyers, and academics. And I noticed that all of the men wore expensive suits, all the women wore fancy dresses and there were very few children. But then I saw a family that didn't fit that description at all.

At the very end of the line stood a father, mother, and four small children. The man wore an open shirt with a red bandanna around his neck, and baggy pants. The woman wore a long dress and scarves over her head and around her shoulders. The kids had dirty faces, the older ones dragging shopping bags behind them over the courtyard's bricks. The family was obviously poor, perhaps homeless. I wondered what they were doing there, where they came from, and how they happened to be in an upper-middle class area like this.

As the family approached the Holy Father, I saw Vatican security people step cautiously forward. Then I saw first the pope and then Monsignor Dziwisz shake their heads as if to signal to the guards to allow the family to approach.

The family came before the pope, the parents with bowed heads, the children looking up at the pope with wide eyes. When they all stood in front of John Paul, the father and mother raised their faces. They seemed very nervous but after the pope, smiling, stepped forward and took their hands, they both began to look more comfortable. They began to talk to the Holy Father, slowly at first, then faster, the words spilling out. The pope listened intently. After a while he replied—not in full sentences, but in phrases, in individual words.

Kathy and I were standing only a few feet away, so we could hear what they were saying. But neither of us could understand a word. They weren't speaking English, of course, but it didn't sound like Italian, either. Claudio, my embassy driver that day, was standing beside us. I asked him what language they were speaking, whether it was some local dialect. "It's not Italian," Claudio said. "I think it must be Romani. They look like that. And they have a special feeling for this pope. They are ignored by everybody, but not by Papa."

Romani is the language of the Gypsies, and for me finding out that they were Gypsies made the scene even more special. I watched even more closely now as the mother held up one of the smaller children. The Holy Father blessed him and then took him from her. He held the dirty-faced little boy close, not worrying that he might get his spotless white cassock dirty. The boy seemed a little scared at first, but then he caught sight of the crucifix on the chain around the pope's neck and began to play with it. "*Con permiso. Es mio* [Excuse me. But that is mine]," the pope said, speaking Italian. Claudio translated. Then the pope, holding the crucifix up to the boy, explained, "This is Jesus. My job is to tell people about him."

Looking around the courtyard, I saw that everyone had formed a circle around the Holy Father and the family, and they were watching this scene unfold. I couldn't help recalling the Holy Father's words inside the church a few minutes ago, quoting Blessed Josemarie Escriva: "God awaits us every day. Be sure of this: There is something holy, divine, hidden in the most ordinary situations, something that each one of us must discover. There is no other way, my children; either we know how to find the Lord in our ordinary lives, or we will never find Him."

A year later, John Paul II canonized the first Gypsy saint, Ceferino Jiminez Malla, a martyr of the Spanish Civil War. Thousands of Romany from all over Europe flocked to Rome to attend the canonization ceremony in St. Peter's Square. For a week before the event, they camped out all over Rome, in the parks and on the streets, cooking food over open fires, playing guitars and singing songs. On the day of the ceremony, I sat with the other members of the diplomatic corps in my usual front-row seat on the steps of the Basilica. But I couldn't help thinking of the scene the year before at that new church in the new neighborhood of Rome. And I couldn't help remembering what Claudio had said that day: "They have a special feeling for this pope. They are ignored by everybody, but not by Papa."

25

TRIP TO SLOVENIA

Seeing him in action in another country

Seeing John Paul II in action on his home court, at the Vatican and in
Rome, was one thing. Seeing him on mine, on his trips to the United
States, was another. But, I'm glad I also got the chance to see him at
work in a "neutral site," and experience for myself the impact he ex-
erts in other countries.

One of my best friends in Rome was Steve Falaz, a very successful
Slovenian businessman. In 1992, when the Vatican became one of the
first governments to recognize the "breakaway" Balkan republics of
Slovenia and Croatia, Steve became his country's first ambassador to
the Holy See.

The Holy See's recognition of Slovenia and Croatia had provoked
an outcry, both from in and around the Balkans, and from a number of governments around the world, including the United States.
Critics charged that the Vatican had jumped the gun in recognizing
those two primarily Catholic countries (of the 1.9 million people
in Slovenia, 1.7 million were Catholic) and that this recognition
had accelerated and made more difficult the eventual breakup of Yugoslavia.

I think there might have been something to that argument, and,
possibly because he based his decision on his own experience in
Poland rather than the much different situation in the Balkans, the
pope might actually have acted too quickly. But whether he did or

not, nobody did more to draw attention to the tragedy unfolding in the Balkans than John Paul II.

As I explained earlier, the pope tried to visit the three capitals of the war-torn Balkans in the fall of 1994. When that couldn't be arranged, he did visit Zagreb in Croatia. He held a special Mass in St. Peter's once to pray for the people suffering in the Balkans that was attended by the entire diplomatic corps. In his homily, the pope delivered one of his most direct criticisms of the European community for not doing more to stop a war in its own backyard. I had never seen the Holy Father look so angry. His voice bellowed, he shook his fist. After the Mass he walked straight out of St. Peter's Basilica, looking neither to the right nor to the left, his face grim. It was clear that he was trying to send the message through the diplomatic corps to their governments that: "The pope really meant it on this one."

It wasn't until May 1996 then that the Holy Father made his next trip to the Balkans, this time to Slovenia. Steve Falaz had been pushing for the trip ever since his country had declared its independence. He was thrilled that the Holy Father was finally coming, and he invited me and a handful of other ambassadors to go along.

On the morning of Friday, May 17, we arrived at Ljubijana International Airport, where the Holy Father was welcomed by Milan Kucan, the president of the Republic of Slovenia, and other members of the government. The welcoming ceremony was similar to those I had seen and been a part of in the United States—a warm reception by an enthusiastic delegation and series of speakers. When it came time for him to speak, the Holy Father called Slovenia "the crossroads of people and bridge between the Slav, Germanic, Latin, and Hungarian worlds," and declared how pleased he was "to be in your country for the first time, in this land studded with the countless bell towers, churches, and chapels that bear witness to your people's deep Christian roots."

As usual, the pope got a rousing ovation from the crowd. After he was escorted to his car, the rest of us were led to our cars, and the motorcade that followed brought us to the next event, a vespers service at the beautiful seventeenth-century Cathedral of Ljubijana. We were shown to our seats at the front of the church. When the Holy Father entered, just before ascending to the altar, he stopped at the front pews of the church to greet the handful of ambassadors from other countries who had come with him to visit Slovenia.

"I am so pleased you could join us in this country with so much history and that has suffered much pain," he told us. "I am glad you could experience the blessing that Christ has given us of seeing people remaining faithful to the church despite all the obstacles they face." I couldn't help but think that the pope must have been thinking of his own country, Poland, as well as Slovenia, when he said these words.

During the service, attended by several thousand of Slovenia's priests and nuns, the Holy Father repeated that theme. He referred to the "trials to which the Slovenian people have been subjected" and the importance of the clergy to the people: "Dear Brothers in the Episcopate, dear priests, dear religious, dear brothers and sisters: the Slovenian people need you. Europe and the world need you, because they need Christ." Although the ceremony inside the church had been geared to the country's clergy, when we got outside we saw that the square surrounding the cathedral was packed with ordinary citizens. They cheered when the Holy Father emerged from the church, cheered louder when he waved and blessed them, and chanted his name as the motorcade pulled away.

The Slovenian trip was very similar, in some ways, to the pope's triumphant trip to the United States six months before. On Saturday, the Holy Father's seventy-sixth birthday, he celebrated Mass at the Stozice Racecourse in Ljubijana on a huge altar topped by a triangular white canopy. Many young people were in the crowd of over a hundred thousand, and they cheered, chanted, sang and waved banners just like the young people in New Jersey, New York, and Baltimore had. The only difference was their language. The pope himself delivered all his speeches in Slovenian. The other ambassadors and I were provided with translations throughout the trip.

The Holy Father's homily on Saturday had to do with the celebration of the Ascension of Christ to Heaven. But once again he talked at length about the "serious trials" suffered by the people of Slovenia, especially in recent history, which he listed as the two world wars, "the violent Communist revolution," "the suffering caused by foreign occupation," and the "scourge of civil war, in which brother took up arms against brother." As John Paul closed by issuing greetings in a number of languages, including Serbian and German. "I repeat today what I said at the beginning of my ministry of the Chair of Peter," he said. "Do not be afraid! Do not be afraid of Christ; have faith in him and in his love." He closed by saying: "Dear brothers and sisters . . . you, too, must cross the threshold of hope together with me, with your bishops and priests, and with the whole church."

On Saturday afternoon, the Holy Father met with Slovenia's bishops at the College of St. Stanislaw Kostka. Afterward, he had a brief meeting with the prime minister, which was followed by a speech to young people who filled a private airport in Postojna.

On Sunday morning, we all left Ljubijana for Maribor, where the pope celebrated an outdoor Mass before hundreds of thousands of people. It was an overwhelmingly hot day. I remember thinking that if those of us in the VIP group were uncomfortable, after having been driven out to the Mass from our hotel a short time before it started, the rest of the audience must feel much worse since most of them had arrived before dawn. They were men, women, and children of all ages, and they had walked for miles carrying blankets, food, and probably not enough water. Some of them came in horse-drawn carts. Many mothers pushed baby carriages with scarves shielding their children from the hot sun. The long walk and the difficult conditions didn't seem to affect their enthusiasm, though. People were singing, waving flags, and saying prayers. When the pope's helicopter came into sight, they erupted in a thunderous ovation, and when, a few minutes later, the Holy Father came into view riding in the back of the popemobile, everyone was up on their feet and cheering. It was as if, at that moment, they had forgotten the heat, forgotten what they had gone through to get there—because it was worth every minute of their effort to see the Holy Father.

Instead of being driven directly to the huge outdoor stage with the altar set up on it, the popemobile circled the field a couple of times so more people could see the Holy Father up close. When the car finally approached the stage, I saw that the pope looked exhausted. I wondered if it was just the strain of the trip, the heat, or if he was ill. He slowly descended from the car and shuffled slowly toward the stage, with the Bishop of Ljubijana beside him and hundreds of priests following behind. Before climbing the stairs, though, the Holy Father noticed our group sitting in the front row and stopped to greet us again. "Thank you again for coming," he said, his face drained of color, dark rings around his eyes. And then: "Isn't God good to keep faith so strong alive in this country? The church is strong in Slovenia because people are strong." Looking at him, I wondered how *he* could stay so strong. He was seventy-six years old. He'd been shot, been injured, and his health wasn't good. In all this heat, he was wearing heavy, formal vestments. Yet here he was, making small talk with us—and thanking God for keeping faith alive in this country.

John Paul climbed slowly up the steps to the altar, and then, since he hadn't been able to realize his dream of visiting all of the Balkan countries, he tried to make up for that at this one Mass by welcoming the cardinal of Zagreb and the bishops of Croatia and Yugoslavia. In his sermon, the Holy Father talked about how, in present-day society, there was "a deep need of saints, of people, that is, who through their closer contact with God can somehow make His presence felt and mediate His answer." He also delivered words of praise for "many Slovenian mothers [who] have gained a special mention in the nation's history by offering a significant model of consistent Christian living." By the end of his sermon, despite the electric fans that had been set up around the altar, the pope was drenched in sweat. But he kept going, saying the rest of the Mass, handing out Communion, even singing along with the choir.

Before praying the *Regina Coeli* at the end of the Mass, the Holy Father spoke to the crowd extemporaneously, and reflected on his visit: "In these days, I was personally able to feel the affection of this people, their deep faith, their unshakable fidelity to the church," he said. "I was also able to admire the beauty of your country, its mountains, hills, and green meadows. God bless this country . . . God bless Slovenia."

Listening to his words and looking around me at the rapt faces of the people of Slovenia, I began to re-think my opinion that the Holy See had been premature in recognizing the independence of this country. How can you justify keeping a country and a people like this away from their faith, away from God?

26

FIFTY YEARS A PRIEST

Two lions of the church, wrestling to show their respect

In November 1996 John Paul II celebrated his fiftieth anniversary as a priest. As part of a weeklong series of events to commemorate the anniversary, a vespers ceremony was held in Paul VI Hall. The Holy Father had asked Catholic priests from around the world who were celebrating their fiftieth anniversaries to join him in Rome, and the hall was filled with priests who had taken him up on his invitation, along with their families, friends, and parishioners who also made the joyful pilgrimage.

At the vespers, the Holy Father sat up on the left-hand side of the stage with members of the papal staff, including Master of Liturgical Ceremonies Monsignor Piero Marini, and the pope's two secretaries, Monsignors Stanley Dziwisz and Vincent Tran Ngoc Thu. When it came time for his homily, John Paul addressed the sixteen hundred priests from eighty-nine countries and five continents as his "dearest brothers in the priesthood, ordained fifty years ago like me." He thanked them for coming to Rome, and reminded them that the "gift we have received" was a "mystery of communion which begets communion." Then the Holy Father reflected on his own life. He spoke about all the people who helped him to find his vocation: his family, his parish in Wadowice, his friends in school and at the factory where he worked, and his confessors—all of whom led him to enter what he called "the clandestine seminary." At one point, he got a laugh from the crowd when he talked about how, when God called their names, "we answered: 'Here I am!'"

After the Holy Father finished speaking several other priests made brief remarks, including Monsignor Feliciano Barreto Castelo Branco of Brazil and Father Edward Kangootui of Namibia. Archbishop Dario Castrillon Hoyos, pro-prefect of the Congregation for the Clergy, presented a gift to the pope from the jubilee anniversary priests. The Holy Father, in turn, presented the gift of a stole to five priests representing all the priests from the five continents. Then Father Anton Luli, an eighty-six-year-old Jesuit from Albania, rose from his seat a couple of rows behind mine and made his way, slowly, up the low stairs to the stage. Everyone knew that Father Luli had spent forty-two of his fifty years as a priest in Communist prisons and labor camps, and everyone's eyes were on him as he made his way to the microphone, his steps slow, his frail body bent. When the elderly priest spoke, his voice was barely audible. Still, everyone could hear him because the place was absolutely silent.

Father Luli spoke in Albanian, but copies of his remarks had been translated and passed out to the audience beforehand. His remarks included a testimony to the priesthood in which he described the joy of the vocation as transcending any suffering it might bring. As he spoke, I looked over at the Holy Father. He was sitting in his chair, his head tipped to one side, one hand on his forehead and his eyes closed. I couldn't tell for sure—even though I was only about ten yards away—but I thought I saw tears running down the pope's face.

When Father Luli finished, he began to make his way back to his seat very slowly, first down the steps, then over toward the center aisle. I turned back to watch the pope again. He raised his head, put his hands on the arms of the chair, and looked over toward where Father Luli had been speaking. He appeared . . . puzzled, as though he'd been expecting Father Luli to come over to him . . . as if he was surprised to see the frail old priest returning to his seat. The pope gestured with his good, right hand. A priest, in a white surplice over a black cassock came over, bent down to him, then walked quickly across the stage and down the steps. It was clear he'd been sent to get Father Luli and bring him back up to the pope. When the younger priest caught up with the older one, he whispered something to him, then took his arm and started leading him back toward the stage.

Father Luli approached the stairs again and seemed to sigh, as if he had just climbed down from a mountain and now he had to climb back up. I wanted to leave my seat and go help him. I think everybody in the place did. But all we could do was watch. Slowly, Father Luli made it back up the steps and shuffled over to where the Holy Father was sitting. As he did, the pope struggled to rise from his chair, rocking back and forth, finally producing the momentum he needed to get to his feet just as Father Luli reached him.

When they met, the Holy Father opened his arms, to hug Father Luli. But the old priest either didn't see him because his head was bowed or didn't feel deserving, and instead tried to go down on his knees to kiss the Holy Father's ring. The pope would have none of that, though. Not there. Not then. Not after all this priest had been through at the hands of the Communists. So he grabbed Father Luli by the shoulders and tried to haul him back up. There they were, up on the stage in front of six thousand people, wrestling, two old lions of the church. It was like a duel. It was as if they were saying to one another: "It is I who have so much respect and love for you." "No, no. It is I who have so much respect and love for you."

They were competing to honor one another. I looked around me at other members of the diplomatic corps. It was clear from how intently they watched and the looks on their faces that if they hadn't understood what being a priest in the Catholic Church was all about before, they surely did now.

On the stage, the pope and the priest were still sparring. Despite all the time he had spent in prisons and labor camps, Father Luli still had enough strength left in him to get down on his knees. Once he did, he went for the pope's ring, grabbing at the Holy Father's hand with both of his. Now the pope had his second wind, and with all the strength left in a body that had suffered more than its share of injuries in recent years, he hauled the Albanian priest up to his feet and hugged him. I mean he really *hugged* him—a great big *bear hug*. For a second there was total silence. Then, like a river coming down from a mountain, a thunder of applause came rolling row after row, from the back of the hall right down to the stage. I looked around and behind me, and I didn't see a dry eye in the house.

After their embrace, the pope and Father Luli spoke to one another. Then they kind of patted each other on the shoulders. Neither of them seemed to want to break it up. Finally, helped by the young priest who had brought him back earlier, Father Luli returned to his seat in the audience. As he passed by where I was sitting, I could see the tear stains on his cheeks, and feel the tears welling up in my own eyes.

After the service, people rose from their seats and walked up the aisles mechanically, as if they had been drained of all emotion. I joined the throng of cardinals and diplomats around Father Luli and was able to shake his hand. The old priest seemed confused at being in the spotlight. I left through a door near the stage reserved for the diplomatic corps, but once outside, instead of heading to where my car was waiting, I went over and stood outside the door that the pope uses. The security people—the plainclothes guys and the Swiss Guards—knew me well by then and allowed me to stay there. I don't know why, but I've always liked to stand by stage doors and watch the "stars" come out. When I was a kid growing up in Boston I used to hang around outside Boston Garden, Braves' Field, and Fenway Park to see the ballplayers come out of the locker rooms after games. As an adult, I enjoy waiting outside the stage door after Broadway shows. In Rome, I just liked to see the pope after these events, to observe his face, to get a sense of what kind of mood he was in.

When the Holy Father did step out the rear door of Paul VI Hall, I couldn't catch sight of his face at first. His head was down, he was walking carefully over the cobblestones of the courtyard. The pope's doctor was with him, as well as Monsignor Dziwisz and two or three other priests. I looked around and saw that Archbishop Tauran and a few other Vatican officials were also there, standing in the background like me, watching curiously. It was as if we'd all realized that this was a special night and we wanted to make it last a little longer.

We were all standing on the far side of the pope's car, a black Mercedes. As he approached the car from the other side, he looked up and saw us and waved. It was a signal that those close to him recognize. When he's tired or in a hurry, he doesn't look up, he just gets into the car and off he goes. But if he stops and looks up, it means he's exhilarated, has some time, wants company. We took his wave as an invitation, and everyone moved forward a couple of steps.

"*A buona sera,*" I said in Italian, smiling.

"A wonderful night," the Holy Father replied in English, smiling back. "Father Luli . . . those priests . . . that priest. Those are the heroes, the real heroes of the church. The soldiers of Christ. We thank God for them."

Then just before getting into his car, the Holy Father raised his hands over his head, clasped them together, and shook them, like a prizefighter who had just been declared the champion.

27

ARRIVEDERCI, ROMA

Glad to be going home, sad to be leaving him

I served as U.S. Ambassador to the Holy See for more than four a half years, somewhat longer than the usual tour of duty. In the fall of 1997, though, I was ready to go home to Boston—though I knew I'd miss Rome and John Paul II.

On September 18, 1997, I had my last official meeting with the Holy Father. Like the first one, at which I had presented my credentials, this one took place at his summer residence at Castel Gandolfo, where he stays until mid-September to avoid Rome's summer heat.

Kathy had already returned to Boston to look after our son Ray and to start getting our household back together. My daughter Maureen was the only member of our family with me in Rome. Since the ceremony for taking leave of the Holy Father is less formal than the one at which he welcomes a new ambassador, Maureen and I drove out to Castel Gandolfo in the embassy car, without all the pomp and circumstance we had been a part of in the summer of 1993. We arrived at the town in the Albano hills a little early, and stopped at a café in the town square for cappuccino.

When it was almost time for my appointment, we got back into the car and pulled up to the big wooden doors of the pope's summer residence. The doors opened and the car pulled into the courtyard. Someone from the papal staff, not Bishop Monduzzi but a layperson, met us and brought us inside. We waited for a few minutes in the "holding room" overlooking the gardens and Lake Albano, then, while Maureen stayed there, I was ushered into the pope's library.

The Holy Father met me at the door and gave me a big Italian hug, pressing both of his cheeks against mine. He put his two hands over my hands and brought me over to an armchair, then went around behind his desk and sat down. You present papers from your country's government when you arrive on the job, but there's no protocol that calls for you to submit anything upon your departure. Even so, I gave the pope a letter summing up my tenure as ambassador, similar to the one I had written to President Clinton.

"So you are leaving us, Ambassador Raymond," the pope said.

"Yes, Holy Father," I said. "Rome might be the Eternal City but Boston is home."

"Home is good," the pope replied. I think I detected a wistful note in his voice. "Home is always good. Your memories . . . your family . . . your childhood . . ." I could almost see him going back in his mind to Wadowice.

We talked a little bit about some of the contents of my letter, since I had given a copy to Archbishop Tauran beforehand. I told him how honored I felt at having been given the chance to know him and to know and work with people like Cardinal Secretary of State Angelo Sodano and Archbishop Jean-Louis Tauran, Secretary for Relations with States; Archbishop John P. Foley, president of Social Communications for the Holy See; Monsignor James Harvey of the Vatican's Secretary of State's office; and American Cardinals Bernard Law, John O'Connor, William Baum and Edmund Szoka. I also mentioned Monsignor Tim Dolan, prefect of the North American College. I told the Holy Father that, as ambassador, I had tried to emphasize the many positive areas of agreement between the United States and the Holy See while acknowledging the few, but important, areas where positions were not shared. I recognized, I said, that my tenure as ambassador had not been without controversy. But I believed any controversy resulted chiefly over matters of conscience—and that my thinking on these issues had been reinforced by watching and listening to him these past four-plus years.

The Holy Father listened carefully and patiently. When I had finished, he said, "The United States is a special country, with a special history, but it also has a special obligation. It must always be a people who work for peace and justice for all." I couldn't help but think back to the Holy Father's triumphal visit to the U.S. and how he had expressed that same message in speech after speech.

I asked the Holy Father about the challenges that faced the church. "We look forward to the Jubilee Year," he said, "to renewing our commitment to Christ and one another. We also look forward to visiting the Holy Land and to walking in the footsteps of Abraham."

I didn't want to overstep any diplomatic boundaries, but I asked the pope what he thought was the key to peace in the Middle East. "Jerusalem," he replied without hesitation. "All people, all religions must be able to live there in peace. Jerusalem should not be a problem. It should be an example." He was referring, I knew, to the Vatican's proposal that Jerusalem become an international city, rather than serve as the capital of either Israel or Palestine.

The pope shifted the conversation from world affairs. He asked me about my future, about what my plans were. "You are going back into politics?" he asked.

"Yes, Holy Father, I hope to. I like helping people. I'm thinking of running for governor of Massachusetts. But it will be difficult. I have been gone a long time."

The pope nodded, but American electoral politics was one area that I didn't think he or others in the Vatican really understood. I had the feeling that the pope and other Vatican officials assumed I could just waltz right back to the U.S. and pick up where I left off. I didn't want to tell him how hard it would be or that my identification and agreement with some of the issues he cared most about—notably, the right to life—would be a big obstacle to my ever winning office again.

The pope looked at me very sternly, then. "The pope cannot pray for you to win, Ambassador Raymond," he said.

"Oh, I know that Holy Father," I replied quickly.

But even more quickly, John Paul interrupted me, saying, "But maybe the pope can pray that you do not lose." Then, his face brightened into a big smile and we both laughed. He was pleased with his joke and the effective way he had set me up for it.

"We are going to miss you in Rome," the pope continued, seriously now. "You made a lot of friends here."

"Maybe more friends in Rome than in Washington," I replied. This time it was *my* turn for a joke.

But the Holy Father didn't laugh. He knew I was referring to the run-ins I'd had with the White House and State Department over what I considered matters of conscience. "You had a difficult job here," he said, "particularly over the situation in Cairo and more recently over this law they are trying to pass. (He was referring to the ban on late-term "partial birth abortions" that President Clinton vetoed despite my recommendation that he allow it to become law.)

"We know it was difficult for you," he continued. "Very difficult. But you did your best. You were loyal to your country, faithful to your church, and true to yourself."

I couldn't say anything. I was choked up with emotion. For him to say what he did showed me once again how clearly he understood everything that went on around him—even what a U.S. ambassador had been going through. We sat there for another minute or so, then the Holy Father made the sign of the cross and we both prayed.

The door from the other room opened and Maureen was shown in. She had been with Kathy and me in Rome for the whole four and half years and had met the pope numerous times, so she was pretty comfortable with him by now. We stood up, and the Holy Father walked over and took Maureen's hands in his.

"But it is time for the young people to lead," he said to her, "to do the work of God in whatever field of life they choose." Then the pope blessed us. It was time to go. Before I did, the Holy Father hugged and kissed me—in the Italian style, on both cheeks. "You may be leaving Rome," he said, "but know that you always have a friend here."

28

BRINGING THE SPIRIT TO ST. LOUIS

And calling for an end to capital punishment

In January 1999, I got my first post-ambassador opportunity to see the Holy Father when he made his fifth visit to America as pope. He was coming from Mexico, where he had just finished a five-day trip that culminated in a Mass celebrated before more than one million people in Mexico City. As it turned out, almost one million people were going to see him during the thirty hours he spent in St. Louis, his only stop in the United States before returning to Rome. It was the biggest crowd to turn out in that city since Charles Lindbergh returned after piloting the *Spirit of St. Louis* in the first solo flight across the Atlantic Ocean in 1927.

On the eve of the pope's arrival, there were stories in the newspapers and on television suggesting that he would "challenge" the United States on specific issues such as abortion—and on more general themes, like a continued commitment to a compassionate society. My sources at the Vatican told me that the pope was also going to zero in on another hot button issue—capital punishment. I was glad to hear it.

The death penalty is one of the most volatile, divisive, and emotional issues in American politics, and has been since the U.S. Supreme Court ruled it Constitutional in 1976. Since then, there have been more than five hundred executions in the United States. Polls show that over 70 percent of the American people favor capital punishment, so it's hard to find politicians willing to take on the issue.

Even somebody as supposedly liberal as Bill Clinton, a graduate of Georgetown University and Yale Law School, and a Rhodes scholar, ducked the issue. When he was running for president in 1992, he actually left the campaign trail to go back to Arkansas to witness the execution of a retarded man. Capital punishment is also a difficult issue to talk about. It's hard to be rational over an issue charged with emotions—such as pain, anger, and revenge. It is particularly hard when the media focus on the obvious harm inflicted on victims and their families by criminals but pay little attention to the more subtle harm done to a society that kills human beings, guilty though they might be.

But if anybody could change the prevailing environment regarding capital punishment, if anybody could bring rationality and morality to what is an otherwise irrational debate, it was John Paul II. That's just what he did when he came to St. Louis.

It wasn't the first time the Holy Father had spoken out against the death penalty. Once, I remember, while I was ambassador, the pope held a briefing in Rome for the diplomatic corps to talk about the church's position on the issue. My understandings of his remarks were that he all but ruled out the use of capital punishment. A few hours later, though, at a reception at the North American College, I ran into a well-known, media-savvy, conservative American theologian who had a different impression.

"Well, it's good to see the Holy Father still believes there's a place in the world for the death penalty," he said.

"That's not what I heard," I replied. "I thought he said just the opposite."

Somewhat condescendingly, I was told that I'd missed the pope's point. I didn't argue. I'd seen countless instances where conservatives and liberals interpreted something the Holy Father said the way they wanted to hear it. So I bided my time until a clarification was made. I didn't have long to wait. A few weeks later, the pope's spokesman, Dr. Navarro-Valls, quoting from the pope's encyclical *Evangelium Vitae,* said that in today's world, cases where capital punishment was justified were "very rare, if not practically nonexistent." A few days after that, I attended a conference in which Cardinal Ratzinger was asked to give an example of an instance when capital punishment was permissible. "I can't think of one," he replied.

I looked forward to hearing the Holy Father clarify the church's position to the American people.

As a former Ambassador to the Holy See, I was part of the official welcoming delegation on hand to greet the pope when his plane landed at Lambert Field. I watched as he was helped down the steps of the plane by his good friend Archbishop Justin Rigali of St. Louis, and was then greeted by the president and Mrs. Clinton, and my successor as Ambassador to the Holy See, former U.S. Congresswoman Lindy Boggs.

Once again, it was an awkward time for the pope and the president to be meeting. When they met in June 1994, the two leaders had been on opposite sides of the population control issue. This time, President Clinton was on trial in the United States Senate over the Monica Lewinsky affair. But the pope wasn't going to change his schedule because of the president's problems, and the president wasn't about to duck greeting the pope, so both of them went about their business as if nothing was wrong.

The president escorted the Holy Father off the landing field and into a National Guard hanger at the airport that had been converted to a reception hall. Blue plastic curtains hung from the ceiling, and red-white-and-blue or yellow-and-white bunting was draped everywhere. As the two men entered the building, the crowd began the usual chant of "John Paul Two!—We love you!" The president and the pope moved to the speaking area, where a large number of seats up front were reserved for people with disabilities. The Holy Father never forgets this special constituency wherever he goes.

President Clinton spoke first. He talked about what an honor it was to welcome the Holy Father, and praised him for "helping people to find the courage to stand up for themselves—from Africa to Asia to the Western Hemisphere." When he finished, the president got what could only be described as polite applause. When the pope stepped up to the microphone to speak though, the cheering echoed off the metal walls of the converted airplane hangar.

The pope looked tired after five grueling days in Mexico. As usual, though, he brightened up once he began to speak. He said how happy he was to be back in the United States and to be visiting "historic Saint Louis—the Gateway to the West," and he called for everyone in the United States "to reassert the spirit of Saint Louis and to reaffirm the genuine truths and values of the American experience." But then instead of merely resorting to feel-good ceremonial rhetoric, the pope got right down to business, reminding people of things they might not want to remember. He opened with a reference to the Dred Scott case, tried in St. Louis, and described how "the Supreme Court of the United States subsequently declared an entire class of human beings—people of African descent—outside the boundaries of the national community and the Constitution's protection." Then he warned: "America faces a similar time of trial today. Today, the conflict is between a culture that affirms, cherishes, and celebrates the gift of life, and a culture that seeks to declare entire groups of human beings—the unborn, the terminally ill, the handicapped, and others considered 'unuseful'—to be outside the boundaries of legal protection."

The previously boisterous crowd was subdued now, listening carefully to his every word. This was the kind of serious talk I had come to expect from this man, the kind of hard truth I expected from him and loved him for telling. He closed his short but powerful speech by saying: "Only a higher moral vision can motivate the choice for life. And the values underlying that vision will greatly depend on whether the nation continues to honor and revere the family as the basic unit of society."

The amount of applause the pope received—expecially compared to the applause for the president—was almost embarrassing. I was sitting in the second row, right behind the American cardinals. Sitting next to me was another "cardinal," Hall of Fame baseball great Stan Musial, an old friend of the pope. "He's still got his fast ball," I said to Musial, nodding toward the pope.

"I wouldn't want to hit against him," Musial said, "especially in front of this crowd. It feels like he's playing at home."

The pope received terrific applause from the two thousand people in the hangar. Then he and the president retired to a private room for a brief meeting. When they came out, the two men, along with Mrs.

Clinton and Archbishop Rigali, stood in a receiving line on a low riser set up at one end of the hangar. We all lined up, everyone eager to have the opportunity of having a few seconds with the Holy Father. When it came my turn, the president introduced me to the Holy Father, a switch from our former roles.

"You remember Ambassador Flynn, Your Holiness," he said.

"The ambassador is our very good friend," the pope said, "and always will be."

The pope looked around then, as if expecting to see other members of my family. But when he didn't see them, he asked: "How is your family? Your wife? All your daughters? Your sons, especially your oldest boy?"

"Everyone is well, Holy Father," I said. "We all think about you and pray for you."

"Give them my prayers, also," the pope said. "Especially for your son."

I knew that I didn't have much time, but there was something that I especially wanted the Holy Father to hear. Lowering my voice a little, I said, "I have heard you might preach against capital punishment, Holy Father. Someone must do it, and as usual it is you. I just want you to know it is a message we need to hear in this country."

"Thank you, Ambassador," he said. "America is beautiful. She must always choose life instead of death. Only God gave us life. Only God can take it away."

The Holy Father blessed me, and I started to move away. But as I did the pope grabbed my hand, pulled me back, and pointed to the words on the sweater I was wearing: "Pontifical College of North America."

"Rome and the Vatican are still part of you," he said.

"And always will be, Holy Father," I replied.

As I stepped away, I noticed U.S. Representatives Dick Gephardt and Patrick Kennedy in front of me in line. They had been talking to Mrs. Clinton, but had turned to eavesdrop on my conversation with the pope. Both of them had stunned looks on their faces, as if they didn't know that you could talk to—and with—a pope like that.

The papal party left the airport. Before the Holy Father took on the issue of capital punishment, he stopped first to reconnect with one of his favorite constituencies—America's young people—at the new Kiel Center in downtown St. Louis. I had known the old Kiel Auditorium very well from my basketball days. In fact, it was after a game there against the St. Louis Hawks that the legendary Red Auerback, reluctantly he said, named me as the last guy to be cut from the Boston Celtics prior to the 1964–65 season.

I had been given a pass from the archbishop's office that allowed me to roam around backstage, and I was only a few feet away when the Holy Father met one of America's biggest heroes of the moment, St. Louis slugger Mark McGwire. When the pope came out into the auditorium—riding on the little white golf cart that served as the popemobile—the twenty thousand young people filling the place rose out of their seats and gave him a standing ovation. They were jumping up and down and screaming and waving yellow scarves. I had forgotten the excitement the man generated, especially among young people, and it was good to see it again.

As usual, the pope hammed it up at first. When he walked out onstage, one of the first things he did was to use his cane to take a fake slap shot, in tribute to the hometown St. Louis Blues hockey team. The crowd loved it, and so did the pope. He was the fun-loving grandfather everyone is glad to see. Soon enough, he got serious, though, and began to deliver the pull-no-punches straight talk to the young people that they loved him for. I watched the expressions of deep interest on the faces of those sitting around me as they listened closely to the pope's every word.

"Christians are always in training," he told them. "Freedom is not the ability to do anything we want. Rather, freedom is the ability to live responsibly the truth of our relationship with God and with one another." They got a kick out of him when he mentioned the home run duel of the previous summer between Mark McGwire and Sammy Sosa, but the pope asked that they use McGwire and Sosa as examples to achieve a goal more important than succeeding in sports— "the goal of following Christ, the goal of bringing His message to the world." He closed by giving the young people a word of encouragement. "The pope believes in you, and he expects great things of you."

After the event, which was more like pep rally than anything else, I followed some of the thousands of young people to an impromptu march to the St. Louis Arch. They were all bubbling over with enthusiasm, laughing and singing while waiting for their buses to pick them up and bring them home after what for many of them had been a chance of a lifetime, a chance to see the pope.

The next day was the main event. John Paul II celebrated Mass for more than a hundred thousand people inside the Transworld Dome in what some called the largest indoor event in the history of the United States. Buses from parishes all over the Midwest had rolled into the city before dawn and had begun unloading people five hours before the event even started. Joining the pope were two hundred and fifty bishops and more than a dozen cardinals. This was an older crowd— and a much more reserved and serious event than the festive one held the day before. But just as he had the previous day, the pope was in great form and this was the occasion he had chosen to declare his unconditional opposition to the death penalty.

John Paul called on Catholics to be "unconditionally pro-life" and said that he was renewing "the appeal I made most recently at Christmas for a consensus to end the death penalty, which is both cruel and unnecessary." Even those who commit "great evil" must be spared, the Holy Father said, explaining that "modern society has the means of protecting itself without definitively denying criminals the chance to reform." It was both a reasoned explanation and an emotional plea designed to help put an end to a practice that was no longer needed to protect society. And yet, it seemed to make some people in the audience nervous. I noticed quite a few people looking around, trying to get a sense of the general reaction the pope's message was eliciting, as if they had to check with their neighbors before deciding how they felt about it.

That was just the start of the pope's campaign against the death penalty. The mass appeal. Next came the personal approach. Immediately after the Mass, the pope had Cardinal Sodano invite Missouri governor, the late Mel Carnahan, to meet with him at Archbishop Rigali's residence that afternoon. The governor did, and that's when John Paul II asked him, face-to-face, to spare the life of the man who had been scheduled to be executed that day: Darrell Mease, a fifty-two year-old career criminal convicted of a triple murder. It was a gutsy move by the Holy Father. Governor Carnahan had a mixed record when it came to capital punishment. He had commuted four previous executions and granted indefinite stays for another three. But he had also allowed twenty-six executions to go forward. A few years earlier, he had spurned a previous request by the pope to spare the life of a man who had been convicted of killing a state trooper. John Paul II was putting the governor on the spot, but he was putting himself on it, too. To have such a public plea for mercy rejected could be seen as an embarrassment to the pope and a slight to the church. But the life of a man—albeit a murderer—was at stake, and the pope was willing to give it a try.

I don't know how things were left between the Holy Father and the governor at the end of their meeting, but I do know Governor Carnahan attended the pope's next event, a prayer service at St. Louis Cathedral. The Holy Father's message at this service focused on ecumenism as well as compassion. Muslims and Jews had been invited to attend, and the executive vice president of the St. Louis Rabbinical Association participated in the ceremony. In his homily, the pope described power as "service, not privilege. Its exercise is morally justifiable when it is used for the good of all, when it is sensitive to the needs of the poor and defenseless." Then he told the audience, "America, if you want peace, work for justice. If you want justice, defend life. If you want life, embrace the truth—the truth revealed by God."

After the service, the Holy Father walked from the altar to the area in front of the first rows of pews. He blessed a group of children. He spoke with some of the religious leaders attending. Then, with all eyes on him, he walked over to the front pew where Vice President and Mrs. Gore and Governor Carnahan and his wife, Jean, were standing. After greeting the vice president and his wife, he turned to Governor Carnahan and asked him again—publicly this time and in front of the vice president and everyone else there—to "have mercy on Mr. Darrell Mease."

Governor Carnahan had a tough decision to make. Was he going to say no to the pope and risk looking insensitive and uncaring? Or was he going to say yes and risk looking like he'd buckled under pressure and mixed church and state? No one knew which way he'd go; it wasn't long until everyone found out.

John Paul II's TWA Boeing 767 left St. Louis for Rome at 8:25 P.M. Half an hour later, by his own admission, Governor Carnahan decided to honor the pope's request, and when he announced it the next day his decision made news, not only in St. Louis and the rest of Missouri, but across the country and around the world. It was the first time that the pope had been able to win a reprieve for a criminal in the United States sentenced to death—and hopefully the first step in dismantling what he has called this "cruel and unnecessary punishment."

29

THE MILLENNIAL POPE

Leading the church into another century

The next time I saw Pope John Paul II wasn't as a diplomat or a politician, but as a journalist. For the last year, I had been hosting a daily talk show on National Catholic Family radio and was about to begin a daily cable television show on the American Catholic Network.

Carrying press credentials instead of diplomatic ones, I returned to Rome in April to experience some of the Catholic Church's Jubilee Year 2000. It was my first time back since leaving my post as ambassador, and I was pleased—and surprised—at the some of the changes that had taken place during that time. Rome had undergone a real sprucing up. An amazing amount of construction and restoration work had been completed in a very short time to help the city accommodate the expected increase in visitors during the holy year. Churches and public buildings shone after having years of grit and grime removed. The streets were clean. Even the notoriously bad traffic seemed to be moving more quickly, thanks to the construction of a few new streets and tunnels.

Walking to St. Peter's, I was glad to see the sidewalks crowded with pilgrims. I knew how important the Jubilee Year was to the Holy Father, and I was glad to see that all the evidence pointed toward it being a big success. When I got to the square, though, I was startled by another change—rows of airport style metal detectors were set up between the columns of the colonnade, and everyone had to pass through them. Rome's police department is responsible for providing security in St. Peter's Square, and I guess the excitement—and tension—generated by the pope's recent trip to Israel and the prospect of increased crowds for the Jubilee Year had caused them to make this change.

After passing through the security check, I entered the square and was directed by various ushers up front to the *reparto speciale,* the seats up on the *sagrato,* or temporary stage, erected over the steps of St. Peter's and surrounding the temporary altar. I found my place on the right-hand side of the altar, the side on which stood the statue of St. Paul. I looked around at the others in my section. For the most part, they were well-dressed adults, many with cameras, only a few with children. Off to the right was a large group of young men in military uniforms. To their right, closest to the doors of St. Peter's, were groups of schoolchildren with their teachers and chaperones.

I looked up at the sky. It had rained steadily for the past two days, rained harder, in fact, than I had ever seen it rain in Rome. From the look of the dark clouds hovering just above the dome of St. Peter's, it appeared as if it were going to rain again. For the pope's sake, as well as the sake of those in the audience, I hoped the rain would hold off for a few hours at least. Unfortunately, it didn't. Instead, it began to fall, lightly but steadily, prompting most of those in the crowd to raise their umbrellas.

St. Peter's Basilica is closed to the public before, during, and for a short time after the audiences, its iron gates closed across the tall wooden doors. Just outside the gated door on the left, a choir stood, and they began to sing, the music spreading throughout the square over loudspeakers. I looked up at the facade of St. Peter's. It, too, had been beautifully cleaned and restored since I'd last seen it.

The singing stopped. I watched a small platoon of Swiss Guards in their red, yellow, black, and blue uniforms march out on the landing of St. Peter's and stand at attention, a signal that the Holy Father would appear soon. As if on cue, the rain stopped and the sun came out. People closed their umbrellas and, smiling, looked up at the clearing sky. Down below in the square, a burst of applause broke out from the area near the *Porto di Bronzo,* the bronze doors, of the Apostolic Palace. Everyone stood up.

Looking down into the square, I saw the little, white, boxy popemobile make its way out from under the colonnade. In the back stood the Holy Father, dressed in gold vestments and wearing a gold miter on his head, holding on to the white roll bar with his left hand and waving and blessing the crowd with his right. I'd forgotten the feeling of excitement he generates, the reaction he elicits from the crowds of people who come from all over the world to see him. "Papa! Papa! Papa!" the crowd chanted. As the popemobile reached each section, people stood and waved and jumped up and down, creating throughout St. Peter's Square the equivalent of the wave you see in baseball parks in the United States. By the time the popemobile turned up the sloped, semicircular stones that form a ramp to the top steps of the basilica, everybody was on their feet, cheering.

The vehicle pulled up alongside the altar covered by the red-fringed canopy and stopped. Fold-out steps were lowered from the back of the car and the pope prepared to get out. The crowd fell silent, watching. Gingerly, without help from either newly-named Bishops Stanislaw Dziwisz or Jim Harvey, who stood on either side of him, the Holy Father made his way down the steps, then shuffled over to the altar, leaning on his crozier as though it were a crutch. It was only when he sat down on a throne-like chair to one side of the altar that the crowd seemed to heave a collective sigh of relief and the cheers began again. It was clear that the pope had become much more frail since I had seen him last, more than a year before in St. Louis. Cardinal Jean-Marie Lustiger, Archbishop of Paris, recently had broken the taboo against discussing the Holy Father's health, describing the pope as "becoming more and more a prisoner of his own body," and I remembered how John Paul had once confided to me: "The pope is old. He is too old." But that had been in October 1994. Now he was presiding over the Jubilee Year of 2000.

With the pope sitting in his chair flanked by Bishops Harvey and Dziwisz, who were standing, the ceremony began. An announcer introduced the groups from all over the world attending the audience. Young people cheered when they heard the name of their group announced. Then a series of readers—men, women, young people—stepped to the microphone at the front of the platform and, in different languages, read the Epistle for the day. A priest read the Gospel: the story of Christ's baptism by John the Baptist. After the readings, the Holy Father prepared to read his commentary on this Gospel story. A priest appeared at the pope's side and adjusted the flexible, thin-necked microphone so that it leaned over his chair. The crowd, already quiet, grew even more silent. It was as if, knowing that the pope's voice was not as strong as it once was, they had to listen that much harder to be sure to hear his words.

The Holy Father spoke first in one language, then another. His voice was hoarse and a little slurred, but gradually, as he spoke, his words became clearer and stronger. The pope read from a sheaf of papers he held in his left hand, which I noticed was not shaking, despite the Parkinson's disease from which he suffered.

I looked around at the rapt audience. Everyone acted as if they could understand every word, even though they were obviously waiting for him to speak in their own language. I looked up at the now clear sky, then behind me at the Apostolic Palace. Most of the windows in the palace were open, and people stood at them in twos and threes. I had never noticed this before at an outdoor audience. I wondered if even the people who worked for him had begun to take advantage of every opportunity to see him and to hear his words. The Holy Father began to read his commentary in English. When he said, "At the River Jordan, the manifestation of the Divine Persons authenticates the mission of Jesus," all I could think of was his own recent mission to the River Jordan—at age seventy-nine and nearing the end of his papacy, but still engaged in the hard work of healing mankind. He finished by saying, "Being reborn in the baptismal waters, we begin our journey of Christian life and witness." I thought of his journey, his life, as a witness for Christ.

The audience ended with the master of ceremonies again reading the names of the various youth groups attending from around the world. Once more, as their names were read, the young people cheered. This time, the Holy Father waved and blessed them. That provoked more cheers, which prompted the Holy Father to blow kisses to those in the audience. That, in turn, led the whole crowd— estimated the next day in *L'Osservatore Romano* at fifty to sixty thousand people—to cheer even harder. The service ended with more singing by the choir. The pope himself joined in the singing, his voice strong even if, as he had joked to me once, "it was more like praying only once."

The formal general audience was over. After the audiences, the pope had always tried to greet as many people individually as possible. I wondered if he would do that now, with his health in decline and after presiding over a two-hour ceremony in unsettled weather. I watched as Bishop Harvey approached with a questioning look on his face, then saw the pope nod his head twice, decisively, as if to say, "Yes, yes."

Bishop Harvey turned, then, and signaled to the ushers, who arranged people in three separate lines. The first line to move forward to meet the seated pope was made up of "dignitaries"—men in fine suits, women in fashionable dresses. The second was made up of brides in white wedding gowns and grooms in black suits, who took turns kneeling before the Holy Father to have him bless their recent marriages. The Holy Father had a kind word, a smile, or a touch for each and every one of them. Then came the third line, the pope's favorite, the line of the disabled—adults and young people. They came forward one by one and knelt down. The pope blessed them, put his hands on their heads or caressed their faces, shook hands with them, and let them kiss his ring.

One of the last in this line was a girl of seven or eight. She had a difficult time walking but she managed to reach the Holy Father and kneel down in front of him without any help. The pope put his hands on her bowed head and blessed her, and then the little girl struggled to her feet. But then, before turning to go back to her seat, she impulsively bent over and kissed him on the cheek. The pope's face broke into a wide smile. He blessed the girl again, then reached out and squeezed her hand. As she turned to go back to her place, I saw the look of thrilled excitement on her face, the same look I had seen on so many people lucky enough to get so close to this pope. Some are already calling him "John Paul the Great" because of the impact he's had on the church and the world. Personally, I'll always think of him as "the People's Pope," because of the effect he has on people—in both large crowds and one by one.

After blessing the last child in line, the pope rose to his feet. With

Bishops Dziwisz and Harvey escorting him, he made his way slowly from the altar area. The Holy Father was obviously tired, his face was drawn, and his step was even slower than it had been earlier. The pope's car—the black Mercedes, not the popemobile—had been brought up onto the landing in front of the basilica. John Paul paused before getting in, as if summoning his last bit of strength. He made it into the backseat and then stood up, his head and shoulders protruding through the sunroof, his hands holding on to a special handle installed for just that purpose. The Mercedes slowly made its way around the perimeter of the *sagrato* and those of us in the *reparto speciale* stood and cheered. The pope waved and blessed everyone, turning from side to side. Just as the car drew alongside where I was standing, the pope turned and looked in my direction. He spotted me, and his head tipped back in surprise. A big smile spread over his face. He nodded his head vigorously, as if to say, "Yes, yes!" Then he blessed me.

The car carried him away, descending the slope from the basilica down to the square below, where it was the turn of the people there to receive the pope. Everyone was on their feet, many even standing on chairs, trying to get a better view, trying to take pictures. They cheered and chanted, "Papa! Papa!" The car made its way through the crowd until, finally, the pope disappeared between the columns of the colonnade.

30

LOOKING BACK THIRTY YEARS

And reflecting on John Paul II's legacy

Five months later, as the Jubilee 2000 celebration was coming to an end, I was in Rome again, this time as guest of and guide for a group of veterans from Boston who were also visiting Nettuno, the military cemetery for U.S. soldiers killed in Italy during World War II.

My first opportunity to see John Paul II came on Sunday, October 1st, when I attended the canonization ceremony for the church's newest saints. Among them were Mother Katherine Drexel, a Philadelphia heiress who became a nun and devoted her fortune and her life to helping African-Americans and Native Americans; and two other nuns, Guiseppine Bahkita, a one-time Sudanese slave who became a member of the Sisters of Charity in Italy, and Maria Josefa del Corazon de Jesus Sancho de Guerra, foundress of the Servants of Jesus of Charity and the first Basque to be named a saint.

The most controversial of the new saints, however, were the one hundred twenty martyrs from China, most of them killed during the boxer Rebellion in 1900. Even though none had died under Communist rule, the current Chinese government denounced many of the new saints as "henchmen of imperialist aggression," and called the pope's decision to canonize them an "open insult"—made even more so by the fact that the ceremony happened to fall on China's National Day, "celebrating" fifty-one years under Communism.

The canonization ceremony was to be held outdoors in St. Peter's Square. It was a gray, drizzly day. I got there early and made my way up to my seat three rows from the altar. I saw that in addition to the flowers decorating the altar and stage four tapestries had been hung from the second floor balconies of the basilica. A likeness of the new saints from America, Sudan, and the Basque province were displayed on three of the banners. The fourth, for the Chinese martyrs, was a yellow banner on which a picture of a cross was surrounded by red letters proclaiming these saints "sacred martyrs."

As I waited for the ceremony to begin, I was greeted by a number of old friends: the pope's photographer, some of the Swiss Guards and a number of church officials, including Cardinals Joseph Ratzinger and Roger Etchegaray. Etchegaray had just returned from a conference in Beijing and we spoke about the controversy over naming these saints. The cardinal said, "Sometimes doing the right thing isn't the most popular thing to do"—a theme of John Paul's that I had learned by heart. "But you can't imagine how much this means to those suffering in China," he added, "people who have never been acknowledged until now."

At 10 o'clock, the choir began to sing, a signal that the pope was being driven up from the Apostolic Palace, and brought up through the crowd. Because my view was blocked by the umbrellas held by almost everyone, I couldn't see the Holy Father, but I could hear the roars from the crowd of over 100,000 get louder, a signal that the pope was approaching. It wasn't until the popemobile pulled alongside the *sagrato* that I saw John Paul. He was wearing green vestments and a gold miter on his head. As he made his way down from the car and over to the altar, I couldn't help but notice how much more frail he had become since April. He looked pale and tired and his body was bent even more than it had been a few months before. But as he took his seat to the left of the altar, I couldn't help but reflect on how he had pressed on in these months—defying the challenges of old age and poor health.

Once again, John Paul had presided over the arduous Holy Week services in Rome. He had canonized yet another Polish saint, Helena Kowalska, a nun known as Sister Faustina, and beatified two of his successors, the much-loved John XXIII and the controversial Pius IX. He had visited Fatima on May 13th,—the anniversary of the day Our Lady first appeared to the three children there and of the day in 1981 that he himself had survived an assassination attempt. The Holy Father chose that occasion to reveal to the world the long kept "third secret" of Fatima—that there would be just such an attack on a "bishop, clothed in white."

John Paul had also continued to speak out on issues of social and economic justice. On May Day, he opened a Jubilee of Workers festival in a suburb of Rome by telling the thousands in attendance, "All must work so that the economic system in which we live does not upset the fundamental order of the priority of work over capital. Globalization is a reality present today in every area of human life, but it is a reality that must be managed wisely. Solidarity too must be globalized." A few weeks later, he had lunch with Rome's homeless.

He had continued to be the conscience of the world, calling for the forgiveness of Third World debt, criticizing the economic embargoes against Cuba and Iraq, arguing that the only solution to peace in the Mideast was to make Jerusalem an "international city" open to people of all faiths. Even as his body was failing, his mind was never more active. At eighty years old, he was still speaking out on issues of morality and science, endorsing organ donation and transplants, but condemning cloning and stem-cell research on human embryos.

John Paul had continued to reach out to the whole world, welcoming two million young people to Rome for the largest World Youth Day so far one day, addressing a group of senior citizens in St. Peter's Square on another. On the latter occasion, sounding like Father Damien, he'd said, "The Church still needs *you*, needs *us*. Precisely because we are old we have a specific contribution to offer to the development of an authentic culture of life." The Holy Father also continued to look to the future. Plans were being made for a visit to Armenia and the pope had again expressed the desire to visit the holy city of Ur in Iraq.

John Paul rose from his chair now to preside over the canonization ceremony, which was beautiful—and and somewhat unusual, since it included singing, dancing, an offering gifts in straw baskets by African Catholics dressed in traditional costumes, and an incense-bearing procession by Chinese Catholics also dressed in their traditional garb. Peering between the umbrellas, I watched the Holy Father, back in his armchair, follow the liturgy closely. This was what he was all about, I realized, reaching out to everyone—especially to the poor, to women, and to the oppressed—to share the word of Christ. Too often John Paul II had been portrayed, especially by the Western media, as some kind of reactionary old man, opposed to change at all costs. Today's ceremony showed how wrong that characterization is.

The Holy Father said as much in his sermon, delivered in a slow, sometimes slurred voice that, as usual, gained strength as he went along. "Today," he said, "the people of God, scattered across the whole earth, is gathered here today, from Asia and Africa, from America and Europe." He credited Mother Katherine Drexel with helping "to bring about a growing awareness of the need to combat all forms of racism through education and social services." He called Guiseppine Bahkita a "shining example of emancipation," and noted that, "in today's world, countless women continue to be victimized, even in developed modern societies." He prayed that the example and intercession of Saint Maria Josefa "help the Basque people to leave aside violence forever." Referring to the Chinese martyrs, he explained that "the celebration is not the time to form judgments on these historical periods," but he also declared, "Today . . . the church intends only to recognize that these martyrs are an example of courage and integrity for all of us and do honor to the noble Chinese people."

After the ceremony, the pope delivered his regular Sunday address. He dedicated most of it to a defense of the controversial document recently issued by Cardinal Ratzinger, prefect for the Congregation of the Faith, upholding the primacy of the Catholic Church. But rather than let Cardinal Ratzinger take all the heat, the pope took it himself. He called the document "close to my heart," and explained that "our confession . . . isn't arrogance that deprecates other religions but an expression of joyous gratitude." He also explained in his sometimes blunt but always honest way that, "A dialogue without foundations is destined to degenerate into empty words." As usual, John Paul showed that he would never resort to empty—or wasted—words.

When the service ended and the pope had gone, many people remained in St. Peter's Square despite the continuing rain. They huddled in small groups near the doors of the basilica or under the wings of the colonnade. I stayed around, too. At one point, I looked up at the *loggia,* the central balcony of St. Peter's. Today, it was flanked by the banners to the new saints, but sometime in the not too distant future, I knew, it would be the place where the announcement: "*Habemus papam*" (we have a pope) would be made—when John Paul II's successor was named. Politician that I am, I couldn't help but reflect on the candidates, the list of *papabili*.

Two of the old friends I had just talked to were on that list. Joseph Ratzinger, prefect of the Congregation for the Faith, was one. He is a German and has been said to be John Paul II's theological "soul mate." Roger Etchegaray, a French Basque and former president of the Vatican Council for Justice and Peace, was another. He has served as John Paul II's international troubleshooter and was someone with whom I worked to set up a system through which the United States could work with the church to deliver aid to victims of famine, war, and other disasters. Angelo Sodano, the Cardinal Secretary of State, was also on the list. I had worked closely with him, and privately sympathized with the tough job he had, since John Paul II often acted as his own secretary of state, foreign minister, and press secretary rolled into one. Camillo Ruini, Vicar General of Rome, was also a candidate and someone I saw often at the various church events throughout Rome.

Francis Arinze of Nigeria, president of the Pontifical Council for Interreligious Dialogue, might be the best bet in terms of someone who could bring Catholics from all over the world together. If he is chosen, he would be the first pope from the third world in modern times. Jean-Marie Lustiger, Archbishop of Paris, whose life story is almost as compelling as Karol Wojtyla's, was also being talked about. He was born a Jew, his mother died at Auschwitz, and he converted to the Catholic faith of the French family who raised him. Two South Americans were candidates—Dario Castrillon Hoyos of Colombia, prefect of the Congregation for the Clergy, and Alfonso Lopez Trujillo, president of the Pontifical Council for the Family. Both were seen as "hard-line conservatives." Lopez Trujillo had taken part in that "tongue-lashing" the diplomatic corps received over the Cairo Conference. I remember Carlo Maria Martini, a Jesuit, telling me, "I'm the liberal candidate, I guess," at his residence in Milan one day.

I got to know Lucas Moreira Neves, O.P., of Brazil when we both received honorary degrees from Providence College, and he used to come for breakfast at my residence while I was in Rome. I would have loved to see him become pope, not just because we are friends, but because he's such a strong advocate for the poor. Unfortunately, his health recently forced him to step down as prefect of the Congregation for Bishops. His successor in that post, Bishop Giovanni Battista Re, served for years as basically the pope's chief of staff. Re was one of the first Vatican officials to greet me when I arrived in Rome. We worked closely together over the years and shared a number of good meals and even better conversations.

I don't really know Dionigi Tettamanzi of Genoa, except that he is said to be a "moderate," or Godfried Daneels of Mechelen-Brussels, supposedly a more "liberal" theologian than Ratzinger. I do know Chrisoph Schonborn, O.P., of Vienna—the editor of one of the Holy Father's "pet projects," the new Catholic catechism—since he was a Dominican priest I saw a lot of in Rome.

I knew it was foolish, though, to engage in the American political pastime of trying to pick a "winner" from the supposed "favorites." There's a saying at the Vatican that "he who goes into the conclave as a pope comes out a cardinal." There is, frankly, no way of knowing whom the cardinals, guided by the Holy Spirit, will choose. But I did know this: The shoes of this fisherman would be hard to fill.

The next day, with the rain continuing, I was back in St. Peter's Square, attending a special audience for pilgrims who had traveled from all over the world to attend the previous day's canonization ceremonies. There were more Africans and Chinese in the huge square than I'd ever seen gathered there before, their enthusiasm hardly being dampened by the steady rain. Once again, I got there early and made my way to my seat up next to the altar. Once again, the pope received the warmest of receptions from the crowd. Just as on the previous day, he referred to the church's newest saints and the examples he hoped they provided to the faithful. While he spoke, in the various languages of those assembled, I looked out at the square below. Some people say that the twin, semi-circular colonnades extending out from St. Peter's represent a key being inserted into the lock of the basilica.

Others say that they are arms reaching out from the church to welcome all souls. As I pondered the symbolism, I couldn't help thinking of the legacy John Paul II would leave.

He has served longer than any pope in the 20th century, and longer than all but a handful of popes in history. During that time, he has reinvigorated and redefined the papacy, becoming the most well traveled, most visible, and one of the most outspoken popes the world has ever known. He has issued thirteen encyclicals, written countless letters, and made thousands of speeches all over the earth, calling on millions of people to love God and one another, respect life, support the family, help the poor, and pay less attention to themselves and the temporary pleasures of this world and more to others and the timeless rewards of the next. If God grants him a little more time, John Paul will soon have appointed nearly every member of the College of Cardinals. He has already created 447 saints, compared to the 302 created in the five hundred years before he assumed the chair of St. Peter. As Cardinal Ratzinger had joked to me the day before, "When he gets to heaven, the pope will already have a lot of friends there."

John Paul II has been a CEO, a foreign minister, an evangelist, and a pastor all rolled into one. He has reached out to other branches of the Catholic Church and Christianity. He has reached out to other faiths, especially the Jewish faith, but also to Muslims and to people in the Far East. He has made the Catholic Church stronger in the present and for the future, but he has also apologized for any wrongs done in the past in the church's name. He has been the most "political" pope in modern history, unafraid to involve himself in the affairs of the world. I think it's kind of ironic that it took an orthodox Jew running for vice president of the United States in the year 2000 to remind the American people that politics and religion don't have to be mutually exclusive. They could have learned that lesson much sooner by following the example of John Paul II. During his tenure, he has met with over 500 heads of state. His role in ending communism is well known, but he has also waged a long and hard campaign against the excesses of the free market. All over the globe, he has involved himself and the church to try to settle wars, provide sustenance, and promote religious freedom and human rights. He has been called the "only truly global leader left," not just because of the office he holds